Anasazi World

Dewitt Jones and Linda S. Cordell

GRAPHIC ARTS CENTER PUBLISHING COMPANY
PORTLAND, OREGON

This book is the catalog of a major exhibition, *Anasazi World*. The exhibition opened at the Maxwell Museum of Anthropology at the University of New Mexico in September 1985. The catalog and exhibition were partially funded by grants from the National Endowment for the Humanities, a federal agency. The Smithsonian Institution Traveling Exhibition Service (SITES) will be circulating the exhibition nationally beginning in March 1986.

Production of the exhibition and catalog has been a cooperative endeavor of federal and state agencies and the exhibition team. The exhibition team consisted of:

Linda S. Cordell, Project Director: Professor of Anthropology, University of New Mexico

Mari Lyn Salvador, Project Coordinator: Chief Curator, Maxwell Museum of Anthropology and Associate Professor of Anthropology, University of New Mexico

Vincent J. Yannie, Exhibition and Catalog Designer: President of Exhibition, Design, Management, Inc., Albuquerque, New Mexico

Dewitt Jones, Photographic Consultant

Alfonso A. Ortiz, Project Consultant: Professor of Anthropology, University of New Mexico

David M. Brugge, Project Consultant: Staff Curator, Southwest Region, National Park Service

Jerry Livingston, Illustrator

Victoria Lucas Olmstead, Graphic Designer

Stephanie Jones, Student Assistant: University of New Mexico

Kayenta Anasazi black-on-red jar, page 31, courtesy of Mr. and Mrs. Morton H. Sachs, Maxwell Museum of Anthropology, University of New Mexico

International Standard Book Number 0-932575-05-6
Library of Congress Catalog 85-71189
Text © 1985 by Linda Cordell. All rights reserved.
Photographs © 1985 by Dewitt Jones. All rights reserved.
Graphic Arts Center Publishing Company
P.O. Box 10306 • Portland, Oregon 97210 • 503/226-2402
Editor-in-Chief • Douglas A. Pfeiffer
Designer • Vince Yannie
Typographer • Paul O. Giesey/Adcrafters
Printer • The Irwin-Hodson Company
Bindery • Lincoln & Allen
Printed in the United States of America
Third Printing

Previous page:
Cliff Palace, framed in a massive sandstone cliff with pinyon and juniper below, Mesa Verde National Park

Contents

Preface

The spectacular ruins of the American Southwest—the cliff dwellings and great pueblos—excite our wonder and curiosity. They are the legacy of a time remote from our own and of a people whose lives we know only in shadowy outline. Delighted by the skills of the ancient builders and artisans, we want to understand how they came to create these enduring and enchanting places. How did they wrest a living from the dry and seemingly barren land? Why, after hundreds of years, did they abandon their villages and disperse? And are there lessons for our own times among the broken tools and fallen walls?

For some of us, the questions have become the focus of lifelong study. Since the ancient pueblo dwellers had no system of writing, we have turned to the science of archaeology to help us read clues from the relics of the "Ancient Ones." As an archaeologist, I have spent a great deal of time in the classroom and in laboratories learning how to discover some of the answers to my questions about the past. My summers are usually spent in the field with my students and colleagues, either locating and mapping archaeological sites or digging in the ruined villages. And every summer season, it seems, there are more new questions raised by our glimpses into the past.

Archaeological fieldwork involves the efforts of many people. Working together, they share the experience of discovery and often discuss problems late into the evening. But, in contrast to the community of camp life, there are always times of silence, solitude, and peace in the open and quite empty land of the Southwest. There are treasured moments spent alone pondering the low mounds of tumbled walls or gazing at an ancient image engraved in stone. At those times one feels a spiritual communion with the past and with the land. It is then that we see ourselves as human beings in the enormity of the universe and of eternity.

It is my hope that this small book will provide a window to knowing both ways of human prehistory. The text describes the story of the ancient Southwest as it has been pieced together by the science of archaeology. The story is an inspiring one; it tells of human creativity and an adaptation to change that extended over a period of eleven thousand years. It is also a tribute to the modern Pueblo Indians, a people who value the past as they embrace the future. The remarkably sensitive photographic art of Dewitt Jones captures the spiritual power of the Southwest—its landscapes, ancient monuments and arts, and the vigor of the Pueblo Indian culture. In his work, Jones provides us with a vision of the Southwest that is truly faithful to the grandeur of the land and its people.

No project of this scope and complexity is possible without the gracious assistance of many institutions and individuals. Dewitt Jones thanks the National Geographic Society for sending him on the assignment that first introduced him to the Anasazi culture. He also wishes to thank Allen Bohnert of the Mesa Verde Research Center, W. James Judge at the Chaco Center, and Chris Judson at Bandelier National Monument for going far out of their way to help him with the project. His special thanks go to the people of San Ildefonso and Santa Clara Pueblos for sharing their culture with him. Linda Cordell especially thanks Janet Hevey, Maxwell Museum of Anthropology; F. Joan Mathien, Chaco Center; and Dabney Ford, Chaco Culture National Historic Park, for assistance in documentation. Thanks also to Emma Mickel, Department of Anthropology, University of New Mexico, for doing battle when necessary and for coping with it all.

LSC
Tijeras, New Mexico
1985

One of the last homes of the Anasazi, the fourteenth-century Puerco Ruin, Petrified Forest National Park

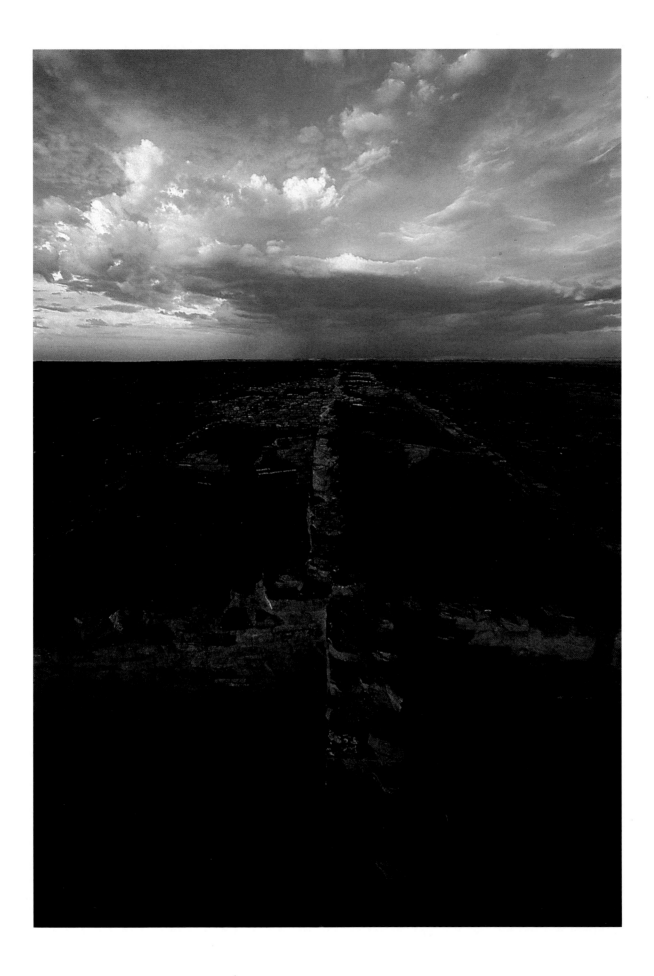

The Anasazi

Ruined villages lie among the barren plateaus of the American Southwest. Abandoned sandstone towers guard the mesa tops. The crumbled walls of silent towns hide in the recesses of shallow caves. Symbols and images carved by human hands adorn the rock cliffs above the plains. Who were the people that long ago deserted these ancient sites? Today we call them the *Anasazi*. At times in the past, their houses and fields extended from the Grand Canyon in the west to the Great Plains in the east, and from central Arizona and New Mexico north into southern Utah and Colorado.

Much of the Anasazi homeland was rugged and barren. The land was bone dry and hot in summer, though subject to sudden storms and floods. In winter the weather was cold and windy and the land covered with snow. Despite the harsh climate and rugged terrain, the Anasazi adapted successfully. For centuries they grew corn, beans, and squash and built the most impressive stone dwellings of prehistoric North America. The modern Pueblo Indians are the descendants of the Anasazi. These Indian people live in adobe and stone villages along the Rio Grande Valley in New Mexico

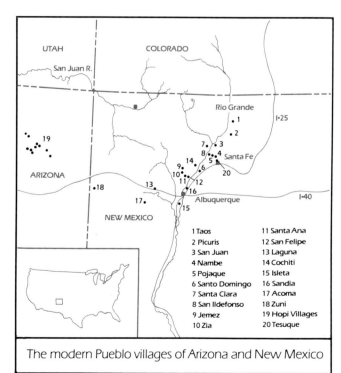

1 Taos
2 Picuris
3 San Juan
4 Nambe
5 Pojaque
6 Santo Domingo
7 Santa Clara
8 San Ildefonso
9 Jemez
10 Zia
11 Santa Ana
12 San Felipe
13 Laguna
14 Cochiti
15 Isleta
16 Sandia
17 Acoma
18 Zuni
19 Hopi Villages
20 Tesuque

The modern Pueblo villages of Arizona and New Mexico

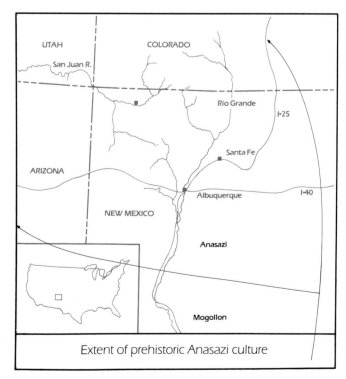

Extent of prehistoric Anasazi culture

and in an area stretching from the Jemez Mountains to the Hopi Mesas of northeastern Arizona.

Some two hundred years after the Anasazi abandoned their western and northern villages, this territory was occupied by Navajo Indians. The Navajo, a mobile people, viewed the ancient pueblo ruins as alien to themselves. The name *Anasazi* is the Anglicized version of a Navajo word for those who built and lived in the ancient villages. This name was adopted by twentieth-century archaeologists who thought it meant "old people" or "those who have gone before." In reality, and much to the embarrassment of archaeologists, the literal translation of the word is "enemy ancestors." Unfortunately no other Indian name exists which can be applied to the prehistoric pueblos of the whole Southwest. It is in part for this reason that the Navajo term is the most commonly used name for this prehistoric Pueblo culture.

Many Anasazi structures have been preserved, thanks to the dry climate and the skill of their builders. Ancient ruins, such as the cliff dwellings of Mesa Verde and Canyon de Chelly, the stone towers of Hovenweep, and the elegant multistoried towns of Chaco Canyon, provide testimony to the Anasazi's sophisticated building techniques. In addition to their skills as builders and farmers, the Anasazi were masters of many crafts. Examples of their artistry can be seen in baskets, cotton textiles, stone and shell jewelry, and pottery which is diverse in shape and painted decoration.

The remarkable preservation of Anasazi relics, made possible by the arid southwestern climate, has attracted archaeologists for more than one hundred years. Their research has supplied us with a richness of detail and interpretation about Anasazi life that is rare for a people who left no written accounts of their world. Within the last ten years, new insights into the Anasazi past have been gained as the amount of archaeological work in the Southwest has increased and as archaeologists have applied newly available techniques to their science.

Our understanding of the Anasazi has also been enhanced by the opportunity to learn from their descendants, the Pueblo Indians. Although the Pueblo people participate fully in twentieth-century American life, they maintain rich oral traditions and a reverence for their land and their traditional way of life. Modern Pueblo artists have earned international renown for their traditional handcrafted jewelry and ceramics, as well as for their painting, sculpture, and English-language poetry. Within the villages, native languages are spoken as is English and often Spanish. The rituals of the traditional native ceremonial cycles are honored as are Christian rituals and ceremonies. Contemporary Pueblo Indian culture combines patterns of behavior learned through more than 450 years of interaction with western European peoples, most recently the Anglo-Americans. The integration of new ways with old gives Pueblo Indian culture a rich texture that cannot be fully understood by outsiders. At the same time, many aspects of Anasazi life are remote and forgotten by the Pueblo Indians themselves. The present and the past are not simple, unchanging reflections of one another. The living people and the silent ruins and relics together allow us glimpses of the Anasazi world.

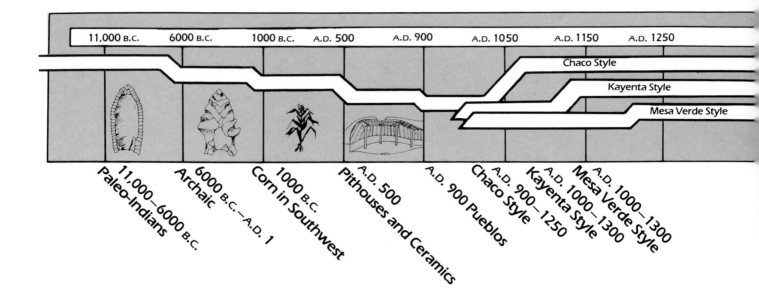

| 11,000 B.C. | 6000 B.C. | 1000 B.C. | A.D. 500 | A.D. 900 | A.D. 1050 | A.D. 1150 | A.D. 1250 |

Chaco Style

Kayenta Style

Mesa Verde Style

11,000–6000 B.C. Paleo-Indians

6000 B.C.–A.D. 1 Archaic

1000 B.C. Corn in Southwest

A.D. 500 Pithouses and Ceramics

A.D. 900 Pueblos

A.D. 900–1250 Chaco Style

A.D. 1000–1300 Kayenta Style

A.D. 1000–1300 Mesa Verde Style

Beginnings

At the end of the last Ice Age, the first American Indians—the remote ancestors of the Anasazi—lived throughout the Southwest. Some of their camps have been found along the edges of ancient lakes, the surfaces of which now are rippled only by sand dunes. Other camping places have been found in rock shelters and caves, and still others lie along stream-cut valleys where no water has flowed for thousands of years.

These earliest Americans, called *Paleo-Indians,* entered the Southwest about eleven thousand years ago. They made their living by hunting very large game animals, such as the now-extinct mammoth and a huge ancestor of the modern buffalo. Paleo-Indian hunters ambushed these creatures along streams and at the edges of small ponds and lakes. Sometimes they stalked them into steep-sided dunes or narrow canyons from which the animals could not escape. The hunters killed these animals with stone-tipped spears or lances and butchered them with stone knives. After the kill, they made spear shafts from the bones and feasted on the roasted meat. Charred bones found in the most ancient campfires and hearths show that these hunters also ate the meat of smaller game, such as elk, deer, and wild sheep. Animal hides were probably used for tents and clothing although these have not survived the millenia. Paleo-Indian

women and children probably gathered the wild plant foods—greens, tubers, berries, nuts, and seeds—in season. They may also have killed very small game for food, such as rabbits, pocket gophers, and squirrels.

During the Paleo-Indian period, the climate of the Southwest was both wetter and cooler than it is today. Vast grasslands, dotted with lakes, provided forage for the bison. Thick stands of trees and reeds grew alongside streams which flowed throughout the year. With abundant food and water, the herd animals could roam nearly everywhere and could readily escape their human predators. For this reason, the Paleo-Indians had to move often in pursuit of their food supply. They did not camp in any one place for very long, and they built only temporary shelters at their camps. Because they lacked beasts of burden and had to carry all their belongings with them, they made and used only a few, very efficient tools. In their travels they quarried natural stones of the highest quality—dense cherts, chalcedony, and some obsidians—to make their spear tips and knives. In order to make the most efficient use of these excellent stone materials, some tools were made to be used for several tasks; for example, a single tool might be made with different edges designed for cutting, scraping, and drilling.

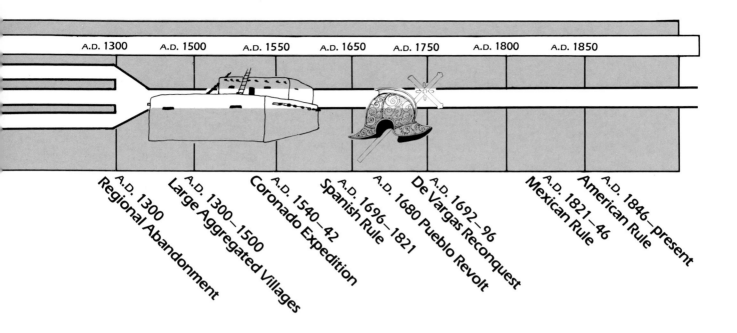

A.D. 1300
A.D. 1500
A.D. 1550
A.D. 1650
A.D. 1750
A.D. 1800
A.D. 1850

A.D. 1300
Regional Abandonment

A.D. 1300–1500
Large Aggregated Villages

A.D. 1540–42
Coronado Expedition

A.D. 1696–1821
Spanish Rule

A.D. 1680 Pueblo Revolt

A.D. 1692–96
De Vargas Reconquest

A.D. 1821–46
Mexican Rule

A.D. 1846–present
American Rule

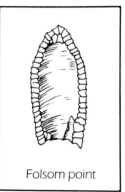

Folsom point

The Paleo-Indians must have known the land and its resources with great intimacy. Through time they would have accumulated the knowledge needed to live off the land comfortably—where to find the best stone, water, firewood, game, and shelter. Generations of adults would have taught their children this knowledge and helped them develop the skills of tracking, stalking, and killing game. Children would also have learned to make fire, prepare hides and clothing, and manufacture tools. Among these tools were the beautifully crafted, incredibly thin, strong, and sharp spear tips that are the most distinctive enduring legacy from Paleo-Indian times. Whatever stories and legends they recounted around their campfires—tales of the hunt, bravery of men and gods—are lost in the shadows of time.

In time, the great continental ice sheets receded to the north, wind patterns changed, and the great inland deserts of the Southwest began to form. The ice age mammoths and giant bison became extinct, and buffalo of modern size gradually shifted their range to the grasslands of the Great Plains. By 4000 B.C., the descendants of the Paleo-Indians had so changed their way of life that archaeologists refer to this later prehistoric culture by a different name—*Archaic*.

Throughout North America the Archaic people continued to hunt, but the game they killed were smaller and of modern form. In the Southwest they hunted elk, deer, mountain sheep, antelope, rabbits, and rodents. They still used stone-tipped spears, but they also used a variety of nets, traps, and snares. Most often the Archaic people camped in the open or in temporary shelters built near streams and ponds. In those places stone tools and small hearths are all that remain. In a few very dry caves, more varied items have been preserved. At one such cave in Chaco Canyon, archaeologists found parts of a wooden spear thrower, fragments of baskets, sandals, matting, cordage, seeds, and seed pods. At a similarly dry and ancient cave in the Grand Canyon, animal figurines made of split twigs were found. Perhaps the figurines were used in magic associated with the hunt, hidden in the dark caves to ensure that there would always be meat to roast over the campfire. No matter what their intended use, they have maintained their remarkably lifelike form for four thousand years.

The quantity of plant material and basketry found in some dry caves and the common presence of grinding stones in Archaic sites suggest that wild plant foods were very important parts of the Archaic people's diet. In addition, charred remains of fruits, nuts, and seeds are frequently found in Archaic hearths and campsites.

Split-twig animal figurine

Throughout much of the Southwest, the climate of Archaic times was slightly wetter than it is today, making the lives of these early hunters and gatherers somewhat easier than we would expect. Still, small game was easily hunted to scarcity in any one location, and the important plant foods were only seasonally available and limited in supply. So the Archaic peoples, like the Paleo-Indians before them, continued to move from one camping place to another to take advantage of different food resources throughout the year.

Archaeologists believe that the size of individual bands of Archaic hunter-gatherers varied during the course of the year, depending upon the particular food resources being consumed. In the late spring, for example, several families traveling together might have moved out into the broad open valleys and flat basins to harvest the early crop of Indian ricegrass. The men might have hunted rabbits or antelope—animals best pursued by several cooperating hunters—while the women filled their baskets with seeds. Later in the summer, such groups of families could harvest cactus fruits and, if there had been good summer rains, a variety of grass seeds. Toward the end of the summer, when it was time to move up into canyons and foothills to gather berries and hunt deer, the group may have split into individual families. Deer are solitary animals best hunted by single hunters, and berries are often sparsely distributed. The smaller group size would have been more efficient.

Later in the fall, individual families and groups of families would converge on certain areas to collect the ripening crops of pinyon nuts. Although the nuts often occur in great local abundance, they are not plentiful in the same place each year. Families might have to travel many miles to the nut crop, collecting as much as they could before the rodents and birds took the rest. The late fall would also be the best time to hunt deer, grown fat on summer browse. The deer would be moving down from the highest mesas and mountains to avoid the coming snows.

Although the men would often be able to hunt during the winter, snowstorms could sometimes make tracking impossible for days or even weeks. Therefore, the late fall was the time for families to store as much dried meat, nuts, and seeds as they could. Winter camps were chosen so as to be close to stored supplies, but a somewhat sheltered location with easy access to firewood and water would also have been an important consideration. In areas where rock cliffs contained shelters and caves, a few families would seek out dry caves for their winter camps. Not all dry caves make good winter camps, however. The preferred caves were those that faced south so that they were exposed to the winter sun. Once a cave had been selected, families would dig deep pits into the cave floors. The pits held enough food to prevent starvation during the worst part of winter.

The hungriest time of year would be in the early spring, before the new shoots and grasses were up and when the stored food may have run out. Game would have been scrawny, if it could be found at all. Perhaps at those times, the groups of families separated, each small household going off on its own search for enough food to make it through until spring was in full bloom.

Archaic point

Archaic people moved their camps throughout much of the year, but their pattern of mobility differed from that of the Paleo-Indians before them. The Paleo-Indians traveled long distances pursuing the large animals that provided most of their food. With a kill of several animals, enough meat might be cached in the frozen ground to last the Paleo-Indian families until spring. Archaic people, relying on smaller game, had to prepare for the coming winter by storing several foods (mostly seeds and nuts) as they became available throughout the year. Given this increased dependence on storage, it became important to stay close to the camp that would be used in late winter and early spring, so that stored foods did not have to be transported over long distances. This change in the scale of mobility is reflected in the types of stone materials used by Archaic people to manufacture tools. While Paleo-Indian tool kits often contained items made of high-quality stone from distant quarry sites, Archaic tools were most often manufactured from locally available stone, even if it was not of the best quality.

Gathering enough seeds and nuts to last through the worst of the winter must have been a difficult chore. The

Woman with burden basket

variable terrain in the Southwest, the marked changes in elevation over short distances, and the differences in temperatures on north- and south-facing slopes combine to create great diversity in the kinds of plants found within the same general area. This diversity of plant types means that large, pure stands of a single plant are uncommon. A group of people gathering ripe seeds and nuts would quickly exhaust the supply in a small area and would have to travel some distance to reach the next small stand. Since the seeds and nuts are ripe for only a short time, and since they are eaten by birds and rodents as well as by people, it would be very difficult to gather both enough to eat and enough to store. Under these conditions, any new plant that could be stored for long periods of time and that required little care would be a welcome addition to the diet. By about 1000 B.C., such a plant became available; this was corn. Although corn initially had very little impact on the Archaic diet, it eventually changed not only the diet but also the whole way of life of people in the Southwest.

Corn was domesticated in central Mexico about 4000 B.C. from a wild grass that grows only in the tropics. The earliest corn was not very productive, but it was a versatile and adaptable crop. With adequate water during its growing season, it could be left untended and would still produce usable ears. When cultivated, weeded, and watered, it would bear large and healthy ears. Yet even when planted in places where the water supply was meager, some plants would still yield small ears containing nutritious kernels. Mature corn could be dried and stored for two or three years; corn that was not quite mature could be harvested "green," roasted, and eaten on the spot. What a boon for the Archaic southwesterners who needed a nourishing food for immediate use as well as one that could be added to their winter stores!

Corn cultivation was not easy or without risk in the seasonally cool and always dry climate of the Southwest. Generally corn will grow successfully, without extra water, only when it is grown at elevations of seven thousand feet and

above. At these elevations there is adequate groundwater retained from melting snow to ensure germination of seeds, and there is enough rainfall during the growing season to bring the crop to maturity. But at higher elevations the temperature is quite cool, and the growing season may be too short for corn to produce mature ears. When corn is grown below seven thousand feet in the Southwest, it generally needs supplemental watering.

At first the corn that was grown in the Southwest was planted in the higher elevations. It was given little care and attention and produced only small ears. The Archaic people may have found it useful to plant some seeds near their winter camps before going off to hunt and to collect the first crop of wild grasses. If crops of wild plants were poor, as they often are in the Southwest, the people could harvest the green corn, as a "back-up" food resource. If the wild crops were adequate, the corn could be left to mature, and the people would have an extra crop to harvest and store for winter. Even though it was treated casually, the corn may often have made the difference between going hungry or having plenty, and sometimes between surviving a long winter or starving.

By about 1000 B.C., Archaic people had incorporated corn into their diet, but they continued to depend mainly on wild foods. In Arizona, New Mexico, and Colorado, tiny cobs have been recovered from dry cave deposits dating to this period. Fragments of squash, another plant that was domesticated in central Mexico, have also been found. Squash produces not only edible flesh and seeds but also rinds that can be used as tools and containers. Somewhat later, by about 500–300 B.C., Archaic people were planting yet another central Mexican domesticate: the common bean. Like corn, beans and squash can be dried and stored, and beans, especially, are an excellent source of protein.

These three crops had been planted and tended for about three thousand years in the tropical areas of Mexico before they appeared in the Southwest. Over time they were adopted by mobile hunter-gatherers in northern Mexico who probably used them as extra sources of food. Seeds were probably passed from group to group many times through the centuries. The Archaic people came to depend on the new plants after two significant changes took place. First, supplies of wild plants on which Archaic life depended became restricted as the population naturally increased. Second, the Archaic people learned to select strains of corn that could be grown with some reliability in the harsh climate of the Southwest by saving the seed of plants that did well in the short growing season with limited water.

Farming never became the exclusive way to obtain food in the Southwest. Gathering of wild plant foods and hunting were always to remain essential. But as crops became more important, sufficient changes in human behavior occurred that the name Archaic, which designates a highly mobile, hunting and gathering way of life, is no longer appropriate. Archaeologists refer to those who followed a largely agricultural way of life in the prehistoric northern Southwest as the *Anasazi.*

Portent of summer rain, a thunderhead, Cortez, Colorado

Petroglyph conveys a message of fertility and natural increase, Galisteo Basin, New Mexico

Careful selection of field locations and
wide spacing of plants allow corn to reach
maturity without irrigation in this Navajo field,
Monument Valley, Utah

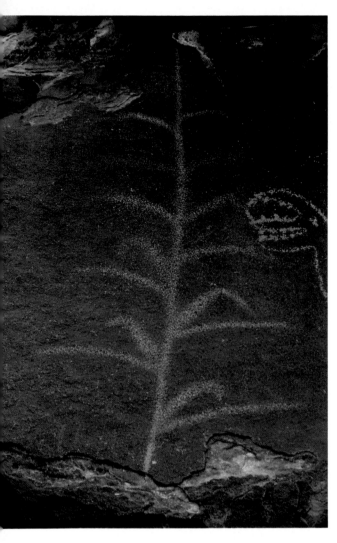

Petroglyph of the staff of life by
a fifteenth-century Anasazi artist,
Galisteo Basin, New Mexico

Painted squash figure reproduced from a
kiva mural recovered in the excavation of
the Hopi village of Awatovi (abandoned in
about A.D. 1700), Museum of Northern
Arizona, Flagstaff

Port in the wall of a unit house could have been used to chart the solstice, Hovenweep National Monument

Previous page:
Ruins at Nankoweap,
Grand Canyon National Park

Moonset, Tower Point Ruin,
Hovenweep National Monument

Migrating birds mark the change in season.
Snow geese, Bosque del Apache Game Refuge,
New Mexico

Fall and winter are the seasons of
animals and the hunt. Elk petroglyph,
Galisteo Basin, New Mexico

Bear petroglyph on the soot-darkened
wall of a small cave near Bandelier
National Monument

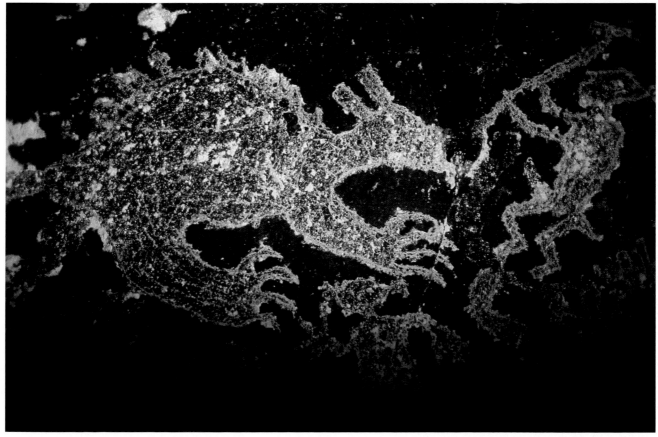

The World Created by the Anasazi

In the parks and monuments of the Southwest, we walk amidst countless ruins of adobe and stone. Abandoned by the Anasazi centuries ago, and silent now, what clues to the past do these ancient buildings hold? The ruins were once homesteads, villages, and towns, noisy with the activities of daily life. In their size, arrangement, and details of architecture, there are keys to an understanding of Anasazi society.

By about A.D. 500, corn, beans, and squash provided a substantial portion of the Anasazi diet. The people spent most of the agricultural season tending their fields and a fair portion of the rest of the year living on stored produce. This dependence on crops required them to stay in one place for long periods of time, and the old mobile life-style gave way to increasing residential permanence. The first durable structures were built to shelter people from the elements and to provide safe, dry places to store food. Archaeologists use the term *Basketmakers* to refer to the earliest Anasazi to settle down. The name is, in part, a tribute to one of their most basic but exceptionally beautiful crafts—plant fiber baskets used to carry and store items of daily life.

Pithouses

The first houses that the Anasazi built were small and dug into the ground to a depth of about eighteen to twenty-four inches. Because they are partially sunken into the ground, they are called *pithouses*. The lower walls form the sides of the excavated pit. The upper walls and roofs of the pithouses were constructed of wood and dried mud. Shallow pithouses were entered through an opening on the southeast side of the house. In deeper houses entry was gained by a ladder through a hatchway in the roof.

Inside the oval or round room, there was generally a central hearth used for heating and some cooking. A small tunnel was dug through one wall of the house and led up to the surface of the ground. This tunnel or ventilator provided a draft for the fire and kept fresh air circulating. A flat stone slab was set upright between the hearth and the ventilator shaft to keep the draft from hitting the hearth directly. Smoke from the hearth escaped through the hatch in the roof. In the floor of the pithouse, near the wall opposite the ventilator shaft, archaeologists often find a small round hole. Although the purpose of these small holes is unknown, archaeologists call them *sipapus*, because some Pueblo Indians use this term to refer to small holes in modern ceremonial rooms. These holes are symbolic representations of the place where, according to Pueblo mythology, the Pueblo ancestors emerged from the underworld.

Clothing, tools, and some corn were stored in the rafters of the house and in small storage pits dug into the floor.

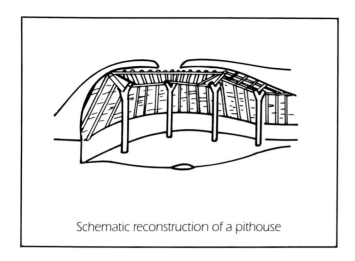

Schematic reconstruction of a pithouse

large, storage pits and began to build rows of aboveground rooms behind the pithouses; they used these rooms for storage while continuing to live in the pithouses. Slightly later on, a double-tiered row of rooms was built. The front rooms served as living rooms, the back rooms as storerooms, and the pithouse continued to be used, perhaps for religious activities or other special purposes. It seems that as the Anasazi became more dependent on crops and as food was stored for longer periods of time, small storage pits became inadequate and larger storage spaces were needed. Food can be stored much longer above the ground than in pits where water seepage and rodents eventually cause too much damage.

Stored corn requires preparation before it can be eaten, and judging from the abundance of manos and metates in the ruins, the Anasazi seem to have ground much of it into flour. Increased dependence on stored corn meant that many hours a day had to be spent grinding it. Any activity or task that requires a lot of time and special equipment is most efficiently done in a space that is exclusively set aside for it. In our own society kitchens are good examples, as are sewing rooms and the workrooms of carpentry hobbyists. The separation and enlargement of different areas for work space, storage space, and living space could not be done in the earth-walled pithouses without the walls eventually collapsing. But separate rooms could be added to the aboveground structures very easily. So, the Anasazi moved to aboveground rooms.

However, most food was stored in larger pits located around the outside of the house. These pits were carefully plastered with clay and sometimes lined with straw or stones to keep them dry. After they were filled, the pits were sealed with stone or clay covers.

The small size of the pithouses suggests that they were each occupied by only a single family. Because the pithouses are so small, it is also likely that many daily activities took place out-of-doors. Hearths and roasting pits found outside the pithouses indicate that much of the cooking was done outside. Some pithouses have low adobe partitions that partially separate about a third of the floor space from the rest of the house. Within such partitioned spaces, small hand-held grinding stones (manos), large slabs with a flat grinding surface (metates), and ceramic storage containers have been found, suggesting that this part of the house was used for some kitchen functions.

Why were these earliest houses built wholly or partly below ground? Certainly it was not an easy task to excavate using only a sharpened, wooden digging stick. In addition, problems of water drainage and seepage must have been common during wet weather. Recent studies have shown that pithouses have superior thermal qualities compared to structures built on the surface of the ground. As long as the floor of the pithouse is below the depth at which the ground freezes in winter, the temperature in the house will not drop below freezing. Also, the earth itself acts as a good insulator; heat is retained in the house, and less fuel is required to keep the house at a comfortable temperature. In summer the pithouse will also be cooler than the outside air temperature. In fact, many solar homes that are built in the Southwest today follow the pithouse principle in having their floors about twenty inches below the surface of the ground.

The pithouse was the most common type of Anasazi dwelling before about A.D. 900. After that time, in spite of their advantages, pithouses were replaced by surface dwellings in most parts of the Anasazi homeland. By the tenth century, most people lived in aboveground pueblos. The reasons for this change in living arrangements are unknown, but some of the reasons can be suggested from what is known about how the change occurred. During the eighth and ninth centuries, the Anasazi in most areas stopped using

Pueblos

The typical Anasazi dwelling is called a pueblo, from the Spanish word for "village." Pueblos share some similarities with contemporary forms of urban housing. Like modern apartment houses, pueblos consist of one or more stories of rooms with shared walls, although they also contain space for outdoor communal work and play and space for religious ritual and ceremonies. Pueblos, however, provided a very different social environment from modern apartment living. In modern urban apartments, neighbors may not know each other. Each household is self-sufficient, going about its activities largely without concern for others and conducting its business, social, and religious activities away from the residence. By contrast, most individuals born into a pueblo would live there all their lives. They would be close kin to many of their neighbors and certainly would know everyone very well. Although some activities, such as cooking, would be done by each household, many tasks such as planting and tending crops, hunting and butchering game, plastering outside walls, and remodeling of rooms would be done by groups of people from several households working together. Many ceremonies too would involve the entire village. Our notions of personal independence and privacy would be completely foreign to the Anasazi.

The ruins of ancient pueblos that we see all over the Southwest today are similar in some ways. In part these similarities are the result of overall similarities in Anasazi construction technology and design. Other resemblances arise from the similar functions these structures served as shelters and homes. The layout of most Anasazi pueblos reflects the need for private household living and storage space, community work and activity space, and ceremonial and ritual space. By joining masses of rooms together and making thick walls of adobe or stone, the Anasazi could provide for separate activity spaces while retaining the thermal insulating properties of the older pithouses.

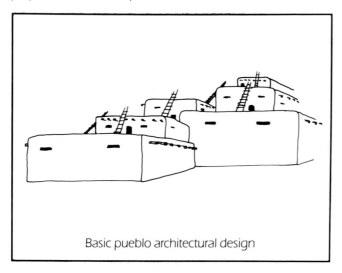

Basic pueblo architectural design

The Anasazi used materials from the earth to build their villages. As a result, the pueblos appear to mirror and blend into the landscapes of which they are a part. Some walls consist of a framework of poles and branches covered with mud (*jacal* construction); others are made of stone masonry with adobe mortar; and still others are built of adobe laid in horizontal courses. Rooms were roofed with log beams called *vigas*, the Spanish word commonly applied throughout the Southwest. Over the vigas were placed smaller branches (known as *latillas*), topped with final layers of reeds, brush, and mud. The inside walls of store rooms or granaries were carefully plastered, and their floors were sometimes covered with fitted stone slabs in order to discourage rodents. Granaries might also be hollowed out of soft volcanic tuff or built on or into sandstone bedrock. Often the Anasazi took advantage of the natural shelter afforded by cliff overhangs and shallow caves; roofs and walls that are protected from the weather require less frequent repairs.

In most pueblos a single household occupied several rooms connected by doorways that could be closed off with matting, hides, or large stone slabs. The largest room, often at the front of the building, served as a general living room. These rooms often contain hearths for heating, light, and cooking, and many have space set aside for corn grinding. The adjoining rooms are smaller and were apparently used for storage; these rooms lack hearths and often have stone floors and clay-lined walls typical of storage areas.

The living rooms in these Anasazi pueblos are smaller than rooms to which we are accustomed. Archaeologists believe that many daily activities were conducted outdoors,

in courtyards, village plazas, or on the flat pueblo roofs. Tools and other items, including whole or restorable ceramic pots, have been found on the collapsed roofs of ancient pueblos, supporting the inference that these areas were used as work spaces. In the larger ancient pueblos, the outdoor plazas were undoubtedly important settings for community gatherings, ritual and secular activity, and work. *Ramadas,* which are roofed structures with open walls, are often built in the plazas of modern pueblos to provide shaded work space, and evidence of similar structures has been found in the plazas of excavated prehistoric pueblos.

The Hopi word *kiva* is used for special ceremonial rooms that are found in all modern pueblos. Among the pueblos of the Rio Grande area, kivas are separate, freestanding, round structures, with floors that lie slightly below the surface of the ground. They are entered by means of a ladder through a hatchway in the roof. In a very general way, they resemble the ancient pithouses. Since such kiva structures are prominent features of ancient Anasazi pueblos as well, archaeologists accept the idea that the old pithouse form was retained, but its function changed from being a domicile to being a locus of religious ritual.

In addition to the general similarity in design between pithouses and kivas, some specific features may occur in both. For example, sipapus, high benches along the wall, wall niches, and deflectors are features of ancient pithouses, ancient kivas, and modern kivas. In modern Hopi villages and the pueblos of Acoma and Zuni, kivas are rectangular, and some are incorporated within the domestic household areas. Nevertheless, they also have special features and are used for ceremonial functions. Access to the kivas is restricted to members of the group belonging to the society affiliated with it. In some villages, clans or special religious organizations control the kivas. In these villages, there are several kivas—one for each organization. In other pueblos, the religious and political responsibilities of the village are divided between two groups that anthropologists call *moieties.* Each group, or moiety, has its own kiva, and the village as a whole will therefore have just two kivas. The number of kivas found in ancient Anasazi sites as well as the design of ancient kivas vary. This variability suggests that there have been changes in the kinds of organizations using the kivas and perhaps in the functions that the kivas served.

A final, spatially distinct area of modern and ancient pueblos is the midden, or refuse dump. Broken and worn-out tools, discarded items, the debris from tool-making, the inedible remains from meals, and the ashes from hearths are among the items found in middens. Some kind of community refuse area is, of course, an important element in maintaining a clean, orderly village. For modern Pueblo Indians the midden is also a sacred place, because the Indians believe that all things from the earth must be returned to the earth. Partly because of the sacred nature of the middens, they were also used as burial grounds by the Anasazi. For archaeologists, the ancient middens provide invaluable information about the foods that were eaten and the kinds of items that were used in the villages over time. It is the worn-out, broken, and discarded items that constitute most of the archaeological record.

The Anasazi and the Natural World

The Anasazi way of life relied on harmony among the people, their crops, and the natural world. The social world of the Anasazi, their tools, and their art changed over time, but the people, their crops, and the world of nature needed to be always in fine balance.

Corn became the fundamental crop to be nurtured and cherished so that the people would not starve. In the arid Anasazi world, water was the most critical resource for corn. All sources of water and all creatures associated with water and rain were important symbols in the Anasazi world and are equally important in the Pueblo Indian world today. Mountains, green and cool, harbor the snow, touch and tether the clouds. All mountains are sacred, and green

Lightning storm, Petrified Forest National Park

boughs from the mountain trees call forth rain and life. Images of storm clouds and lightning capture the essence of summer rain—in murals, on costumes, and on objects that are held during dances for the growth of corn and prosperity. Tadpoles and frogs are from the water and are symbolic of it.

Today corn is planted in ways that protect it and provide each plant with as much water as possible. Cornfields are planted at several places along ephemeral streams so that after a rain, when the water flows, some plants will have moisture before the water evaporates or seeps into the ground. If too much rain falls and the stream becomes a raging torrent, some fields will be lost, but those at the very mouth of the stream may survive. The Anasazi built small stone-check dams across the streams to slow the water and divert some of it onto the fields. They also built rock and earth terraces on steep slopes to slow runoff and allow the water to penetrate the soil. The present-day Western Pueblo farmers plant corn in hills that are several feet apart. The outer plants protect the inner ones from the harsh spring winds, and the spaces between plants help to ensure that they are not competing for water.

All people who depend on crops keep track of the course of the seasons. For the Anasazi this was crucial, because their growing season was barely adequate for corn. The Anasazi had to know precisely when to plant and when continued planting must stop, or the crop would not reach maturity.

Among the modern Pueblo Indians, accurate astronomical observations regulate the ritual and agricultural cycles. Determinations of the exact dates for the winter and summer solstices are particularly important to the ritual cycle.

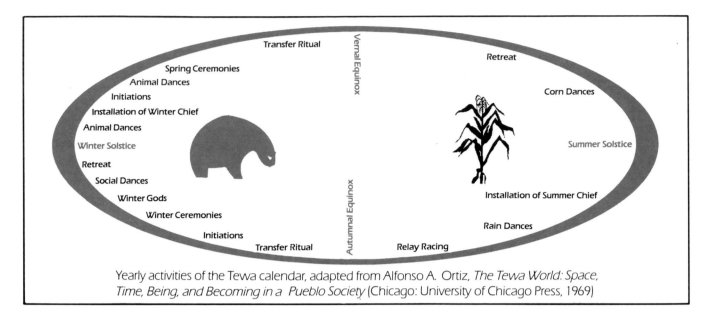

Yearly activities of the Tewa calendar, adapted from Alfonso A. Ortiz, *The Tewa World: Space, Time, Being, and Becoming in a Pueblo Society* (Chicago: University of Chicago Press, 1969)

Since Pueblo ceremonies require preparation time, the astronomical observations must be anticipatory—that is, the people must know days in advance when the solstice will occur. As the time for the sun to reverse its path draws near, religious specialists observe the position of the sun at sunrise or sunset in order to announce to the village exactly when the solstice will occur. Generally the observations are made from a special place within the pueblo or not far from it, and the sun is observed with reference to landmarks on the horizon. At some pueblos, the horizon observations are made from indoors through special windows or ports.

It is certain that the Anasazi also made accurate calendrical observations in advance of the solstices. Astronomers with a knowledge of Pueblo Indian culture and archaeologists with astronomical training have observed that some windows and ports in certain Anasazi ruins can be used to predict the solstices. Working under the assumption that these celestial events would have been of critical importance to the prehistoric Pueblos, these archaeoastronomers are attempting to identify astronomical observation points at other Anasazi sites.

Even though four seasons of the year are recognized in tradition and ceremony within many of the Rio Grande Pueblo villages, there is a more distinctive division of the year into two parts: the spring and summer agricultural time and the fall and winter time of animals and the hunt. These two major times of the year are charted both by astronomical observations and by the semiannual migrations of birds.

Early in November, after the autumnal equinox, the agricultural half of the year is finished, and the fall and winter ritual and social life begins. Animals dominate this time of year, but they are not simply the game animals taken for food. The bear is a very special animal in Pueblo culture. Among many Pueblos the bear is a powerful curer called upon to heal illness. The bear may have been equally important in Anasazi times, since bear effigy figurines have been found in ancient villages. Awesome rock art depictions of bears and bear tracks have also been discovered.

Deer are important game animals in the Pueblo villages today, and judging by the relative abundance of their bones in ancient Anasazi archaeological sites, they were so in the past as well. No food animal is treated casually by the Pueblo Indians. Respect for the animal is shown in ritual before, during, and after the hunt. One kind of ritual is the deer dance in which the animal is impersonated. Deer antlers are decorated with bird feathers that must be newly acquired.

Birds are also significant in Pueblo culture. Their migrations mark the seasons, and the feathers of specific species are required for prayer plumes and ceremonial costumes of all kinds. Some birds have very special relationships to man. The eagle is an honored kinsman and the hunter god of the upper regions. The bones of both raptors and game birds have been found in Anasazi sites, along with those of turkeys. Turkeys had apparently been domesticated by the Anasazi and were used both for food and for their feathers. Warm, light blankets were made from turkey down and turkey feathers. Blanket fragments and even nearly whole examples have been recovered from very dry sites in which preservation is exceptional.

The Anasazi lived in one of the more difficult environments on earth—one that is hot and dry for most of the summer and very cold in the winter. Rainfall, crucial for plant growth, is unpredictable. Sometimes so little rain comes that wild plants and crops alike die. Sometimes too much rain falls at one time and washes out fields before the crop is mature. In some years the growing season extends from spring well into fall. At other times crops are cut down by early frosts and snows.

The Anasazi adapted to their world by combining farming with gathering and hunting. They knew how to track the course of seasons and how to use the resources of the land while conserving them. Their arts reflect a knowledge of and concern for the world of nature. Among their descendants, ancient symbols and ceremonies preserve the traditional knowledge that enabled human society to survive in harmony with the land for two thousand years.

Pueblos Across Space and Through Time

The first-time visitor to Anasazi country may see a sameness in the ancient and modern pueblos. Domestic living space, storage space, open courtyards, plazas, kivas, and middens are features common to all the modern and ancient villages. Yet, as one spends more time among the pueblos, differences become noticeable.

The modern Pueblo Indians share an underlying cultural unity that derives from their long and successful adaptation as farmers and village dwellers. There are differences among the Pueblos, however, that relate to ecology, social organization, and language. Within the pueblos six different native languages are spoken. These are Tiwa, Tewa, Towa, Keresan, Zuni, and Hopi. Although anthropologists do not know precisely how ancient the languages are, most of them seem to go back at least one thousand years. It is likely that those groups speaking the same language have had closer interactions with each other over the centuries than they have had with pueblo-dwellers speaking different tongues.

Somewhat broader, and perhaps more fundamental, differences separate the westernmost Pueblos from the easternmost Pueblos of the Rio Grande Valley. In the western villages, clans are important features of village organization. Each village has several different clans, and the members of each clan are related through women. In these villages children are members of their mother's clan. Households in the Western Pueblos are matrilocal, which means that after marriage a couple will reside in or near the home of the bride's mother's family. In the Eastern Tewa Pueblos, the village organization is based not on clans but on the division of the people into two moieties associated with summer and winter. Children generally join the moiety of their father. Households in the eastern villages usually consist of extended families, related through either the mother or the father. The pueblos where Keresan languages are spoken lie physically between the west and the east, and they also fall between these two extremes organizationally; they have both clans and a moiety division.

In the Western Pueblos, the clans provide political and religious leadership. Leaders of the several religious societies are responsible for the ceremonies marking the annual cycle. In the eastern villages, the moieties provide political and religious leadership and are also responsible for the ceremonial cycle. In the Keresan Pueblos, the clans regulate marriages, as they do among the Western Pueblos, but the moieties are responsible for the kivas and for the ceremonies and dances associated with the kivas. Finally, most ceremonies in the Western Pueblos have to do with bringing rain and ensuring the success of crops. Although rain rituals are also a feature of the Eastern Pueblos, many Eastern Pueblo ceremonies are concerned with curing and healing.

Anthropologists ascribe these differences in social and ritual organization among the Pueblos to differences in environment and ecological adaptation. The Western Pueblo area is generally much drier than the Eastern Pueblo area, and there are few permanent streams in the west. The Western Pueblos rely on rainfall farming far more than do the Eastern Pueblos, who irrigate their fields using water diverted from the rivers. Because rainfall is both scanty and unpredictable in the west, it makes sense that most prayers and ceremonies are offered to bring rain. In addition, the farming strategy that works best in the western area is one in which fields are dispersed in several different kinds of landscape settings. This diversity ensures that even with unpredictable rainfall patterns, the crops in at least some fields will grow to maturity. Among the Western Pueblos, the clans maintain the rights to fields in various settings and locations and carefully preserve stocks of different varieties of seed corn. Clan membership permits each household access to several field settings and to the seed of plants that tolerate different climatic conditions. Because the clan elders are also the village leaders and because the clans can act somewhat independently of one another, leadership as a whole is more diffuse in the Western Pueblo villages.

Among the Eastern Pueblos, there is considerably more security in farming (although disasters do occur in the form of floods or droughts). Fields are not dispersed over the landscape, and each household generally maintains its own fields in the same place year after year. Some of the agricultural tasks related to irrigation, especially the clearing and repairing of ditches and dikes, require the coordinated effort of many individuals. The use of shared irrigation water also demands fair allocation of water and just judgments in disputes over water rights. The more centralized moiety leadership is viewed as providing the political authority to successfully deal with these responsibilities.

The major differences between Western and Eastern Pueblos relate to language and to social and ceremonial organization. These behaviors do not produce tangible remains that are visible in the archaeological record. A possible exception is the difference in the number of kivas in each village, as noted above. The Rio Grande Pueblos generally have two kivas in each village whereas the Western Pueblos have several.

Just as differences among the modern Pueblo groups become apparent on closer inspection, differences in size,

scale, and style are discernible among the Anasazi sites in different regions of the Southwest. Some of this variability may be the result of differences in language, social organization, and ceremonial life, but without written records archaeologists are reluctant to ascribe the differences to these particular aspects of behavior. Rather, archaeologists have described three basic Anasazi styles and have been cautious in drawing inferences about their meaning.

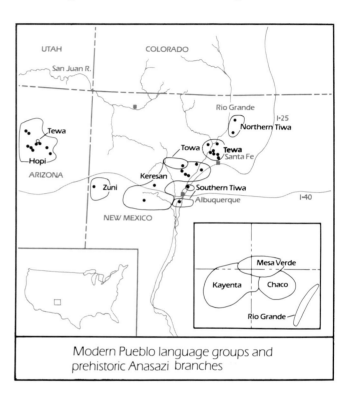

Modern Pueblo language groups and prehistoric Anasazi branches

Kayenta

Archaeologists use the term *Kayenta Branch* to refer to the westernmost Anasazi. These people lived in the area bounded by the Grand Canyon to the west, Monument Valley to the east, the modern Hopi Mesas to the south, and the Canyonlands region of southern Utah to the north. The major Kayenta ruins of Betatakin, Kiet Siel, and Inscription House are preserved in Navajo National Monument, but many smaller or less well-known ruins dot the mesas and cling to the canyon walls of the Kayenta region.

During much of their prehistoric development, the Kayenta Branch Anasazi lived in pithouses or small pueblos that may have sheltered a single extended family or a few closely related families. By about A.D. 900, the Kayenta people were building two different kinds of sites. One kind, found mostly on the mesa tops, consisted of masonry, jacal, and pithouse rooms grouped around a plaza. Sometimes the plaza area was set off by an outer wall. The second kind of Kayenta site is a cliff dwelling. These consisted of a living room, a grinding room, and from one to six storage rooms again built around a common courtyard. Studies of the tree rings of beams used in construction show that these "suites" of cliff dwelling rooms were built at one time.

In the Southwest, tree rings provide archaeologists with their most accurate "calendars" of the events of the ancient world. They also supply precise information about the climate of the past. Each year living trees produce a new growth ring, but in the arid Southwest the width of the ring is determined by the amount of moisture available. Over the years a unique sequence of wide and narrow rings is produced. This sequence can be charted in living trees and then overlapped and matched with the sequence found in wooden beams from increasingly older archaeological sites. By counting back from the present, it is often possible to determine the precise year in which a particular beam was cut. The patterns of wide and narrow rings can also be used to infer rainfall amounts.

It was not until after A.D. 1250 that the large cliff dwellings we most often associate with the Kayenta Anasazi were built. These larger cliff dwellings contained several suites of rooms. This rather standard room-suite pattern of Kayenta architecture indicates that each extended family probably planned and built its own household suite. The fact that the rooms were built at the same time, rather than being added on as needed, also suggests that households did not usually expand to include new members. Perhaps as children grew up and married, they built their own houses.

The Kayenta style of architecture employed unshaped, irregular stones set in abundant mud mortar. The Kayenta Anasazi also frequently used jacal construction for interior walls. From our perspective, the Kayenta Anasazi were rather indifferent architects and masons.

Kayenta communities contain kivas, but these are neither as standardized in form and features nor as numerous as the kivas in other Anasazi areas. Kayenta kivas are either round or rectangular and were entered by a ladder through the roof hatchway. Ventilators, deflectors, benches, sipapus, and wall niches are common but not universal Kayenta kiva features. One feature that links Kayenta Anasazi kivas with modern Hopi kivas is the presence of a series of anchor holes for looms found in some kiva floors. Among the Hopi, cotton cloth is traditionally woven in the kivas by men working at vertical looms suspended from ceiling to floor. Cotton, another central Mexican domesticate, was grown prehistorically throughout much of the Southwest wherever the growing season was sufficiently long. About three thousand textile fragments and a few whole fabrics have been found in archaeological sites that date primarily from about A.D. 1000 to 1400. The Anasazi used a variety of natural dies and weaving techniques (including brocade, twill tapestry, and tie-and-dye) to produce elaborate, dynamically complex designs. The items they made included blankets, sashes, *mantas* (shawls), kilts, and bags.

The Kayenta Anasazi were not only weavers, they also excelled in making pottery. Like all Anasazi pottery, Kayenta ceramics were built up and shaped by hand. The potter's wheel was unknown in prehistoric America. A flat disk of clay was used for the base of the pot, and the potter then shaped ropes or coils of clay and overlapped them to build the vessel wall. Further shaping was achieved by scraping and smoothing the still moist clay with a shaped potsherd or a piece of gourd, wood, or stone. The most common shapes produced were nearly hemispherical bowls and narrow-necked jars, or *ollas*.

Anasazi corrugated pottery vessel

A variety of techniques was used to finish vessels. Sometimes both the inside and outside vessel walls were scraped smooth; sometimes the exterior surface of the overlapped coils was left unsmoothed. Further texturing was done on some vessels by making a series of vertical impressions on the horizontal coils, thus producing a corrugated surface. Plain, coiled, and corrugated jars seem to have been used primarily for cooking and storage. It has been suggested that exterior texturing produces more even heating when vessels are placed over a fire for cooking. The rough exterior also provides a surer grip, reducing the risk of dropping and breaking these much-used kitchen pots.

The surfaces of serving bowls and some water storage jars were decorated with painted designs. Before the paint was applied, a smooth surface was created by polishing the unfired clay with a smooth pebble or by coating the vessel with a solution of very pure clay and water, called slip. Clay chosen for use as slip was often purposefully selected because it took on a specific color during firing. The Anasazi generally used white or gray slips and then applied black painted decoration. Sometimes a red background color was obtained by using iron-rich clays and permitting air to circulate among the vessels while they were being fired. Black paint was derived from a mineral base, such as manganese or iron oxide, which was ground to a powder and mixed with a liquid medium. It could also be produced by boiling a plant such as Rocky Mountain beeweed.

When the painted vessels were dry, they were fired over glowing coals. Today Pueblo potters still use the open-firing technique. On a still morning, a fire is built in an outdoor area that is sheltered from the wind. When the coals are ready, vessels are carefully placed over the fire. If the vessels accidentally touch each other or the bits of burning fuel, smudges and clouds on the pots can result. The fire must be carefully tended and watched until the fuel is gone and the pottery can safely be removed.

Kayenta Anasazi black-on-red jar

The Kayenta Anasazi produced a variety of painted ceramics, but they are best known for very finely painted black-on-white and black-on-red wares. The black paint was applied in very wide lines producing a negative effect such that the design appears to be formed by the white or red background color. The Kayenta also produced beautiful polychrome (black and white on red) pottery.

Throughout most of their prehistoric development (from about A.D. 500 to 1200), the Kayenta Anasazi occupied relatively small and scattered villages. Their territory expanded and contracted through time, probably in response to minor changes in climate which affected their agricultural harvests. The major ruins of Betatakin and Kiet Siel, for which the Kayenta are best known, were not founded until the 1250s. Archaeologists know a great deal about the construction of these two sites. Detailed tree-ring studies have been made to determine the years in which the roof beams of these sites were cut.

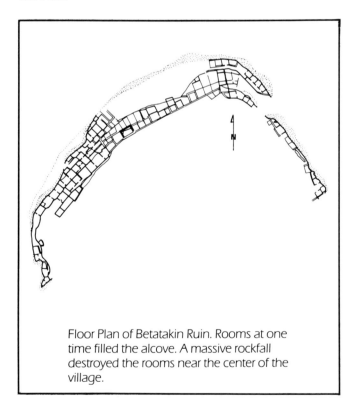
Floor Plan of Betatakin Ruin. Rooms at one time filled the alcove. A massive rockfall destroyed the rooms near the center of the village.

Betatakin Canyon must have been an attractive place for a village. The water table in the canyon is relatively high. Today, aspen, fir, oak, box elder, and willow grow along the canyon

floor, and the vegetation was probably much the same in the thirteenth century. The enormous alcove that shelters Betatakin ruin contains a spring and provides an ideal southeastern exposure. There is some evidence that the rock shelter was used in the 1250s, but little construction took place at that time. Then in A.D. 1267 three room-suites were built. A fourth household was added when another suite was built in 1268. In 1269 and 1272 a number of trees were felled, cut into appropriate lengths for use as beams, and stockpiled. In 1275 these beams were used in the construction of more than ten rooms and at least one kiva. After 1275 rooms were added at a slower pace, until a population peak of about 125 persons was attained in the mid-1280s. The analysis of tree-ring dates indicates that the immigration of new people in 1275 was anticipated and planned for. Subsequent construction was probably undertaken to accommodate internal population expansion. The last cutting date for a beam used in construction at Betatakin is 1286. After that the people seem to have gradually drifted away. What must certainly have been a bustling village was deserted by about 1300.

Kiet Siel, the largest cliff dwelling in Arizona with 155 rooms and six kivas, was founded in about A.D. 1250. The village grew slowly until 1272. Five household units were built between 1272 and 1276, suggesting the influx of a single group of people, perhaps from one village. Thereafter, Kiet Siel experienced gradual population growth followed by a population decline. The diversity in architecture at the site indicates that the residents of Kiet Siel came from several different villages. After only about forty years, the residents of this site, like their neighbors at Betatakin, abandoned their village and moved on.

Eventually the descendants of the Betatakin and Kiet Siel Anasazi joined other immigrant Pueblo groups occupying a series of villages at the southern edge of present-day Black Mesa, Arizona. Today these people are known as the Hopi. In the Hopi language, the cliff ruins of Navajo National Monument are called *Kawestema*, or "North Village." According to the Hopi creation story, Kawestema is the home of some of the Hopi clans, and these sites are still visited today on Hopi pilgrimages.

Mesa Verde

Anasazi of the Mesa Verde Branch occupied southwestern Colorado and southeastern Utah. The ruins of their villages lie mostly in the high mesa country of the San Juan River Valley. The most accessible sites are at Mesa Verde National Park, but Ute Mountain Tribal Park and Hovenweep National Monument preserve fine examples of the Mesa Verde style as well. Mesa Verde-style buildings are distinguished by masonry walls in which each blocky stone was carefully chiseled into the required shape. Sometimes walls consist of a single course of shaped stones; sometimes they consist of double courses. Small kivas are numerous in Mesa Verde-style villages, suggesting that each structure served a few related extended families or small religious societies. The kivas themselves usually lack a bench along the wall, but they have varying numbers of pilasters, a ventilator opening above the floor, and a masonry deflector to shield the fire from too direct a draft.

Two- or three-story towers are fairly common features in Mesa Verde Branch sites. The towers are often connected to kivas by means of tunnels. The function of these towers has been debated by archaeologists for decades, with no conclusive results. Most scholars have been intrigued by suggestions that the towers served either as defensive lookouts or as astronomical observatories. Although both possibilities receive support in some quarters, it has been pointed out that some of the towers were placed in swales or hollows where they offer no vantage point for viewing either the landscape or the stars. Others suggest that, because the towers are often connected to kivas, their form may be purely religious and symbolic. They might, for example, represent mountains—the source of rainclouds and a symbol found in wall paintings of some Mesa Verde kivas.

Kiva jar painted in Mesa Verde style,
Mesa Verde National Park

Visitors to Mesa Verde are justifiably impressed by the cliff dwellings, but in fact, these were among the last structures lived in by the Anasazi in about seven hundred years of residence in the area. Like the Anasazi elsewhere, the Mesa Verdeans first lived in pithouses and later, in small aboveground pueblos. During the earliest pithouse or Basketmaker times, the Anasazi used some of the dry caves in the region for storage and as places to bury their dead. Archaeologists excavating these dry caves have recovered many items, such as sandals and fiber bags, that are normally not preserved in open-air sites. The items found at these dry sites help to complete the picture of the kinds of tools and techniques that were used by the Anasazi. For example, some dry caves have yielded preserved hunting nets that contain miles of fiber. These nets, which were probably used in rabbit drives, combine light-colored plant fibers, such as yucca, with dark human hair to create an optical illusion of openings in the net. Rabbits surrounded by the nets would have tried to escape by heading for the darker patches, but they would still be trapped.

The burial remains found in the caves have often been called mummies, but the name is somewhat misleading. Unlike Egyptian mummies, whose bodies were carefully prepared so that they would be preserved, the Anasazi burials contain natural mummies preserved only by the exceptionally dry conditions of the caves. The burials are vital sources of information about what these ancient Anasazi looked like, what diseases and physical problems they suffered from, and what kinds of clothing they wore or were buried in. The Anasazi were a short people; the men were about five feet three inches tall, and the women were somewhat shorter. They had straight, dark hair and prominent cheekbones. Given the rigors of their lives, it is not surprising that their life expectancy was short. Most people did not live

beyond about thirty-five or forty years of age, a lifespan that is similar to Europeans living at the same time period. For the Anasazi, mortality was especially high among infants and children. The dry caves have preserved the bodies of infants who were buried in their cradles, tenderly covered with soft rabbit-fur blankets. Clothing for adults was scanty by our standards. Men seem to have worn a breechclout or kilt and women a sort of apron. Undoubtedly both men and women wore hide clothing or blankets of feather cloth or fur in cold weather. If moccasins were worn, these have not been preserved, but every adult was buried with at least one pair of finely woven sandals made from yucca, apocynum, and other plant fibers.

During the period between A.D. 700 and 900, the Mesa Verdeans, like other Anasazi, began moving from pithouses to aboveground pueblos. The early pueblos consisted of long arcs of rooms with one or more kivas in front of each arc and a midden beyond. Most of the sites of this type are on the mesa tops and upland sage plains. There the rich, deep soils offer prime locations for agricultural fields. By about A.D. 1000, the Mesa Verdeans began building various water- and soil-control features to protect and enhance their cropland. Within Mesa Verde National Park alone, more than a thousand stone-check dams were built along the courses of ephemeral streams. These slowed the runoff of rain and snowmelt. The dams also trapped soil, so that the area behind these dams provided additional small garden plots. At about this time too, the Anasazi built the stone-lined reservoir that we call Mummy Lake on Chapin Mesa at Mesa Verde National Park. The reservoir, which is fifty-one feet in diameter, was filled by diverting water through a series of ditches to a natural drainage head. Mummy Lake has no outlet ditches; water trapped in the reservoir was effectively impounded there. Archaeologists believe that the reservoir served as a source of drinking water for the several communities built around it.

By the early twelfth century small Mesa Verdean pueblos were spread throughout the region. After about A.D. 1150 or 1200, the population began moving into large, aggregated pueblos, some of which were built in large rockshelters— the cliff dwellings for which the Mesa Verdeans are famous. The reasons for the population aggregation and for the construction of the cliff dwellings are still a mystery. The cliff dwellings do seem defensive, but there is no evidence of hostilities at this time, and many other late twelfth and early thirteenth century pueblos were built in open locations. The sizes of the cliff dwellings cover the full range from one-room sites to Cliff Palace, with its estimated 220 rooms and twenty-three kivas. The large Mesa Verde sites developed in a way that more closely resembles the growth of Kiet Siel than that of Betatakin. There are definable suites of rooms that probably sheltered a single household, but rooms were added on to existing structures and older rooms were modified as household composition changed over time.

In comparison to their Kayenta cousins, the Mesa Verde Anasazi had a large number of kivas in each village. There is really no reason to believe that the Mesa Verdeans were

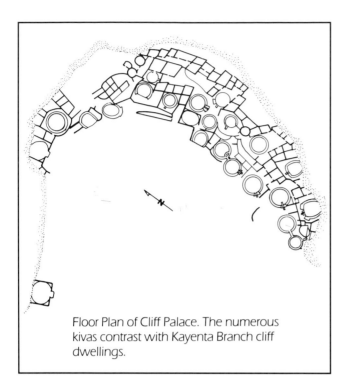

Floor Plan of Cliff Palace. The numerous kivas contrast with Kayenta Branch cliff dwellings.

than five thousand Anasazi villages and nearly one hundred of their large towns. Two hundred years before the cliff dwellings of the Mesa Verde and Kayenta areas were built, the Chaco Anasazi reached a higher level of development than any of their neighbors ever attained. Why the Anasazi came to this desolate land and how they came to build their most impressive monuments there are topics that archaeologists are just beginning to understand.

Today the Chaco style, in all of its forms, is well-preserved at Chaco Culture National Historical Park, a strip of land only ten miles long astride the unimpressive Chaco Wash. Here are the fabled sites of Pueblo Bonito, Chetro Ketl, Pueblo del Arroyo, Pueblo Alto, and others equally grand and striking. These multistoried Chacoan towns, built in the tenth and eleventh

Core and ashlar veneer masonry, Pueblo Bonito

centuries, exhibit careful planning; major architectural units were built at one time by a well-organized labor force. The towns are also quite large. Pueblo Bonito, the largest, contained more than six hundred rooms, and the average among all the towns is 216 rooms. Not only are there many rooms, but the rooms themselves average about twice the size of other Anasazi rooms. The massive walls of the structures taper toward their upper reaches and consist of cored, veneered masonry. In this technique, the load-bearing wall core is composed of rough flat stones set in ample mortar. Each stone is oriented to only one face of the wall and overlaps or abuts the stone on the reverse face. The result is a structurally sound wall. The wall core is then covered on both sides with a veneer of coursed ashlar. The ashlar is often laid on in alternating bands of thick and thin stones, forming various patterns. One architect recently estimated that more than a million dressed stones went into building Pueblo Bonito alone. Despite the appealing design of the ashlar veneer, the Chacoan walls were then covered with adobe plaster or matting.

more religious than other Anasazi; their many kivas may simply indicate that most ceremonies were occasions celebrated by clans or extended families rather than by all the members of a village. It is also possible that the Mesa Verde kivas frequently served as men's clubhouses, places where the men could gather and discuss their business away from the normal turmoil of the household. Kivas often serve this additional function among the modern Pueblo Indians. Today the kivas at Mesa Verde are empty, but when the villages were active, lively places, the kiva roofs would have provided small courtyard spaces where people could work in the open air or simply enjoy the view of the green canyon below their village.

By about 1300 the Mesa Verde villages, like those of the Kayenta area, were silent and deserted. The Anasazi had gradually drifted south toward the upper reaches of the Chama River and Rio Grande drainages. They seem not to have been in any hurry to leave, because they took most of their portable household belongings with them. Perhaps their first new homes were built fairly close to their old cliff dwellings, so that they could visit their former houses and carry away items that were still useful. Eventually the people made their homes among other Anasazi living in the Rio Grande area, where their descendants still reside. Visits to the old homeland quietly ceased, and the cliff dwellings lay empty and brooding above the green canyons.

Chaco Canyon

The San Juan Basin in northwestern New Mexico is a vast, empty land with few trees and very little water. By June the streambeds of its washes are layered with dust. Today flocks of sheep and a few cattle graze on the sparse desert grasses amid eerie rock spires. Yet in the eleventh and twelfth centuries, this desert plain was dotted with more

The town sites face south and contain plaza areas that are almost always enclosed by a low block of rooms or by a high wall. Within every town there are many small kivas, about one for every thirty rooms. Tower kivas, which are circular stone kivas of two or more stories, were sometimes built in the towns. Each town also had one or more great kivas in the plaza area. The great kivas are enormous structures, measuring more than fifty feet in diameter. They have rather standard and unusual features: antechamber rooms, some with recessed stairways leading into the kivas; a central, raised, stone firebox flanked by a pair of rectangular stone vaults; and a high bench and a series of niches along the interior wall. Most of the wall niches were apparently emptied in prehistoric times, but the niches of the great kiva at Chetro Ketl were found sealed with stone. When they were

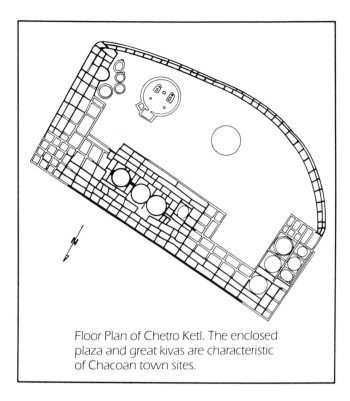

Floor Plan of Chetro Ketl. The enclosed plaza and great kivas are characteristic of Chacoan town sites.

know very little. One of the many continuing mysteries of the Chaco towns is that they have yielded very few human burials, far fewer than either the estimated number of people required to build the towns or the number who could have lived there.

The famous towns within Chaco Canyon are only part of the complex story. Outside the towns are many smaller village sites. These sites contain an average of about sixteen rooms and are only one-story high. The rooms are generally smaller than those of the towns, and they were added on as needed rather than in planned, multiroom additions. The village sites have walls of simple, somewhat irregular masonry. Their kivas are small and unadorned. No single village had its own great kiva, but sometimes a single great kiva served several villages. This was case at the cluster of villages, referred to as *Casa Rinconada,* which lies across the Chaco Wash from Pueblo Bonito. Because the village sites are relatively small and crude in comparison with the magnificent towns, it was originally thought that the villages were the older of the two kinds of communitities. One of the most important findings from the application of twentieth-century dating methods was the discovery that the two community forms were contemporaneous. Some Anasazi were living in rather casually constructed villages while others, just a stone's throw away, were at home in elaborate and highly formal towns.

This pattern of coexisting large and small sites was not limited to Chaco Canyon itself. By about A.D. 1150 this pattern was repeated in some seventy outlying communities spread throughout the entire twenty-five thousand square mile San Juan Basin and beyond. These community clusters are called the *Chacoan Outliers.* They consist of a town site built in Chacoan style with its ashlar veneer, great kiva or tower kiva,

opened, the niches were found to contain pendants and strings of stone and shell beads. The massive roofs of the great kivas were supported either by four masonry columns or by four massive timbers. Huge sandstone disks were used as seatings for the roof-support timbers. Although the roofs of these structures have long since fallen in, the great kivas still reveal the extraordinary effort involved in their construction. When several of these structures were excavated in the early part of this century, some of their roofs, though fallen, were found more or less intact. One of these consisted of more than 350 log timbers. Each of these logs would have had to be carried from forests more than ninety miles away.

Cylindrical pitcher Chaco style

Although wooden timbers and beams were perhaps the most precious items to the Anasazi, the Chacoan towns have also yielded many other "luxury" items: unusual cylindrical vases; human effigy vessels; pottery incense burners; copper bells; trumpets of *Strombus* and *Murex* shell; painted tablets and effigies of wood; macaw skeletons; shell, wood, and basketry items inlaid with selenite, mica, or turquoise; and thousands of pieces of turquoise. Of the particular people who owned or used these elaborate items, we

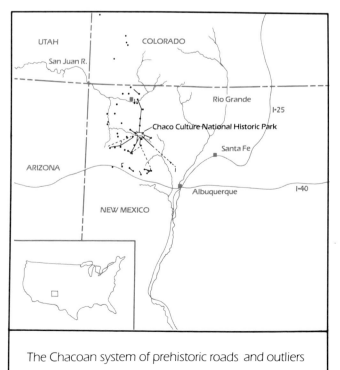

The Chacoan system of prehistoric roads and outliers

and enclosed plaza, and usually an associated group of contemporaneous small village sites.

In the 1970s archaeologists working for the Remote Sensing Division of the National Park Service discovered prehistoric roadways linking the major ruins in Chaco Canyon with the Chacoan Outliers. This discovery demonstrated that these Chacoan Outliers were actually related to the canyon settlements and not simply fortuitous copies of them. The Navajo Indians living in Chaco Canyon had long talked about ancient roads, and archaeologists were familiar with the sophisticated staircases built by the Chacoans. The Jackson Staircase, a well-constructed flight of steps cut into the sandstone cliff behind Chetro Ketl, is a prime example. But the remote sensing crew found that linear features on aerial photographs converged on the canyon from areas as far as forty miles away. Subsequent ground checking and some excavation have, to date, revealed a system of 240 miles of roadway. Most of the roads lead from Chaco Canyon to the Outliers, but some head toward the highland areas around the San Juan Basin. The roads themselves are from about twenty-five to forty feet wide; some are merely shallow swales on the landscape, while others are lined with low berms or stone curbing. Compared with modern highways, the ancient roads are remarkably straight. When a change in direction was needed, it was accomplished by a sharp-angled turn. At the bases of cliffs, the roads stop abruptly, but ramps or steps cut into the stone lead to the top where the road continues.

Since the Anasazi lacked wheeled vehicles and draft animals, the reasons for the construction of these roads remain obscure. It has been suggested that the roads were used for trade, for religious processions, for workers carrying building materials, or for runners relaying messages from one town to another. Whatever the reasons, these roads, like so many other aspects of the Chaco Phenomenon, represent a major investment of labor. It must have take a great amount of energy to dress the million stones used to build just Pueblo Bonito. How much labor was required to construct the other eleven town sites in Chaco Canyon, the more than seventy Chacoan Outliers, and 240 miles of roads in one hundred years? The scale of effort involved is staggering.

When archaeologists discuss the Chaco style, they are talking about an integrated system that linked most of the San Juan Basin through political, economic, and religious ties. This system was of a scale unknown elsewhere among the Anasazi, and from some perspectives, it arose in the least likely place—one of the most barren of all the Anasazi landscapes. Detailed studies of the past environment of the San Juan Basin demonstrate that this part of the world was little different during the eleventh and twelfth centuries than it is today. The tree-ring record does indicate a slight increase in rainfall in the period before and during the height of Chacoan development. This slight improvement in rainfall may have made agriculture somewhat more predictable than it is today, but neither water nor trees were substantially more abundant than they are today. Why, then, the sudden explosion of town planning and building, of production and importation of luxury items, and of road construction?

Theories explaining the growth of the Chaco system are

nearly as plentiful as the ruins themselves, but most are rooted in knowledge of the environment, the Anasazi, and the neighboring prehistoric people. Some archaeologists, particularly those who have worked in Mexico as well as the Southwest, view the growth of the Chaco system as having been directly stimulated by contacts with Mexican civilizations. These scholars point to the presence of some Mexican imports in Chaco sites, notably the macaw skeletons and possibly the copper bells, and some similarities in architectural details, such as T-shaped doorways and plazas. From their work in Mexico, they know that Precolumbian Mexican civilizations thrived on long-distance trade and that many treasured the blue-green stone we call turquoise. Turquoise is a mineral that occurs in the dry desert regions of the world and not in the lush valleys of highland Mexico. Perhaps, then, the Chaco network was established by diplomat-traders from central Mexico who encouraged the Anasazi to provide them with the turquoise they desired but could not obtain closer to home.

Certainly trade or exchange was an important feature of Anasazi life. Clear evidence of trade exists in the form of potsherds that are found well outside the areas in which these ceramics are known to have been manufactured. Was Chaco simply a supply center for turquoise destined for the south? Critics argue that there are no turquoise deposits within more than one hundred miles of Chaco Canyon, the closest source being the Cerrillos Hills near present-day Santa Fe. If the Mexican traders wanted turquoise, why not establish a base among the Anasazi closer to the source or in northern Mexico where the mineral is also found? Another objection raised is that despite a few famous turquoise-encrusted items that have been recovered from archaeological sites in central Mexico, there is simply not enough of this mineral known from Mexican collections to account for the tremendous effort that went into building the Chacoan network.

Another group of archaeologists argues that turquoise was important to the Chaco system, not as an export, but as a medium of exchange among the Anasazi themselves. Because rainfall in the San Juan Basin was both scanty in quantity and spotty in distribution, specific locations in Chaco Canyon may have become centers of surplus food distribution. The town sites of Peñasco Blanco, Pueblo Bonito, and Una Vida are situated at the confluence of major drainages with Chaco Wash. It is argued that, because their locations provided a somewhat more secure supply of water for agriculture, the residents of these towns could grow surplus crops when other villages could not. They may then have pooled and stored their food for later distribution as needed. In theory, pooling resources can be a very effective means of "evening out" the effects of spotty rainfall and unpredictable agricultural yields. It may have been so effective that the system was established throughout the basin. Perhaps the Chacoan towns served primarily as storage centers where, on occasions sanctioned by traditional ritual, resources were distributed to those in need. Were massive give-away ceremonies held in the great kivas? Were the towns themselves maintained by a small group of resident priests and their families in anticipation of periodic Anasazi pilgrimages? This would help to explain the lack of burials found in the towns. Along with this notion, it is argued that turquoise, initially made into ritual objects, became an item of trade itself, reinforcing the ties among Anasazi communities throughout the basin.

Another perspective on the Chaco system emphasizes the kinds of water diversion systems that made agriculture both possible and successful in Chaco Canyon. Chaco Wash was apparently entrenched during the Chaco florescence (as it is today), and therefore it was not useful as a source of water for the Anasazi fields, because the Anasazi lacked lifting devices such as water wheels. Rather, the water for the Anasazi fields came from rainfall runoff that was channeled onto the fields. Water that poured down the bare rock of the canyon walls was funneled into the irrigation system along with water from various side canyons. The Anasazi built diversion dams and ditches to direct the runoff waters to their fields below. The amount of water obtained in this way should not be underestimated, as anyone caught in a summer rainstorm can attest. One archaeologist estimated that during a one-hour summer shower in 1967, 540,000 gallons of water rushed out of a single, small side canyon at Chaco.

Water diversion systems like those described above require constant vigilance and maintenance during the agricultural season. A coordinated labor force would have been needed to clear and repair the dikes and ditches and to distribute water to various fields as necessary. It is argued that some form of social, political, and/or religious control would have been necessary in order to ensure that the right number of people were doing the appropriate tasks at precisely the required times. The Chaco Canyon organizational system is viewed as having been so successful that, when the canyon itself became too densely inhabited to support further population growth, the system was "exported" by colonists who left the canyon to found some of the Outlier villages. The system may also have been adopted by local groups who founded some of the other Outliers.

Whether organized for long-distance trade, for regional exchanges of food, or to control the distribution of water for crops, scholars agree that the Chaco Phenomenon was a unique development in the Anasazi world. This system not only promoted the massive building efforts that have left the ruins we admire, but it linked Anasazi settlements over an enormous area where even today there are few roads and very few towns.

For about a century, the San Juan Basin supported thriving villages and towns. Fields of corn, beans, and squash were green oases below the yellow sandstone cliffs. As the Anasazi tended their crops, traders went from village to village, offering news and gossip as well as their wares. Occasionally, perhaps, traders from the far south were drawn to the bustling towns, offering scarlet-winged macaws for turquoise tessera or beads. At times, processions of men in finely woven kilts and heavy necklaces of shell may have entered the plazas to the measured rhythms of flutes and drums to offer dances for rain and for the good of all the people. Young, swift runners may have preceded them, announcing their expected arrival at each town. Villagers would begin to grind corn and roast meat in preparation for the feasts that would take place after the ceremonies. On the long evenings of winter, men and boys probably gathered by the hearths in the kivas to weave and to make hunting tools, pendants, and beads. While they worked, they would recite and discuss the traditional stories and legends that contained the truths of the Anasazi way of life—the ways of the gods and the ancestors, the habits of mammals and birds, the etiquette of social life, and the organization of the universe.

This high level of integration in the San Juan Basin seems to have lasted from about A.D. 1050 to 1150, quite a short interval in Anasazi prehistory. That the system lasted even one hundred years is remarkable, however, given the overall aridity and low productivity of the basin. Reconstructions of the climate show a period of reduced precipitation in the basin between A.D. 1130 and 1180. Not only was it generally drier than usual, but there were periods of several consecutive years of drought. Tree-ring studies show that Chacoan construction ceased in A.D. 1132. The dry years seem to have broken the system that, for a while, protected the Chaco Anasazi from periodic local crop failures.

Although some of the Chacoans stayed on, many left the region, taking their possessions with them and seeking homes among Anasazi peoples elsewhere. The Anasazi settlements at Mesa Verde continued to thrive, perhaps because their more northern and higher homeland was less affected by the drought. Those Anasazi who remained at Chaco Canyon and in the basin traded ceramics with the Mesa Verdeans and copied Mesa Verde ceramic decorative styles on their homemade wares. Some Mesa Verdeans may have moved to the former Chacoan towns and villages. Both Aztec National Monument and Salmon Ruin on the San Juan River exhibit remodeling in which Mesa Verde-style architecture was imposed on what had been Chacoan Outlier towns. Eventually, as the Mesa Verde area itself was depopulated, Anasazi occupation of the San Juan Basin ceased as well. By 1300 fires no longer burned in the kiva hearths, and spring winds echoed through the deserted Chacoan towns.

Betatakin Ruin, Navajo National Monument

Previous page:
Betatakin Ruin, Navajo National Monument.
The site was settled, expanded, and abandoned
in less than two generations.

Antelope House Ruins, Canyon de Chelley
National Monument

Farview House, Mesa Verde National Park

Massed rooms of pueblos and
settings beneath overhanging rock
afford protection from the elements.

Cliff Palace, Mesa Verde National Park

The view of Cliff Palace
from Sun Temple,
Mesa Verde National Park

Sunrise and a breaking storm, Farview Ruin,
Mesa Verde National Park

In the confines of the cliff dwellings, kiva
roofs served as plaza areas. Spruce Tree
House, Mesa Verde National Park

T-shaped doorway at Cliff Palace, Mesa Verde National Park. The shape is viewed as a possible link to the ancient cultures of Mexico.

Reconstructed ladder entry to a small room hollowed out of soft volcanic tuff, Bandelier National Monument

The formality and planning of Chacoan towns are reflected in series of aligned doorways. Pueblo Bonito, Chaco Canyon

Original tie of yucca defies time, Eagle's Nest Ruin, Ute Mountain Tribal Park

Built of native stones, clays, timbers, and twines, Anasazi ruins echo and blend into the land of which they are a part.

Chetro Ketl, Chaco Culture National Historical Park

Great Kiva, fifty-two feet in diameter, Pueblo Bonito, Chaco Culture National Historical Park

This tri-wall structure behind Pueblo del Arroyo is unique within Chaco Canyon. It was part of a large group of rooms and kivas attached to Pueblo del Arroyo that have been lost to erosion and the Chaco Wash.

Of all the Anasazi styles, the Chacoan was the most formal and elaborate. Chacoan roads linked sites scattered throughout the twenty-five thousand square miles of the San Juan Basin. Chacoan trade extended much further.

This parrot head carved from a single thin piece of wood and painted in lustrous colors was part of a cache of wooden objects recovered in the excavation of Chetro Ketl, Chaco Canyon.

Portion of a prehistoric roadway near Pueblo
Alto, Chaco Culture National Historical Park

These turquoise tesserae, pendants, and beads are from Pueblo Alto, Chaco Canyon. No turquoise occurs naturally in Chaco Canyon. It has been recovered as inlay, jewelry, and workshop debris and is known to have been widely traded.

Cylindrical pitcher Chaco style

Abandonment

The abandonment of the villages and towns of the Kayenta, Mesa Verde, and Chacoan areas has provided a mysterious topic for lengthy discussions among archaeologists and laymen alike. During the first half of this century, scholarly explanations tended to emphasize a single cause, as though a file folder containing all the articles on the puzzle of abandonment could some day be stamped "SOLVED" and put away forever. In fact it is most likely that the abandonments involved a combination of factors.

Traditional Explanations

The devastating effect of a major drought was one of the earliest explanations offered for the abandonments. The drought hypothesis received support in 1929 when A. E. Douglass developed the new techniques of tree-ring dating and climatic reconstruction using tree rings. The tree-ring record showed that a severe drought occurred between A.D. 1276 and 1299. While the reality of this particular incidence of drought has not been challenged, its role in the abandonments has. Scholars have pointed out that the Hopi villages, which are in very dry locations, were occupied throughout this drought when they should have been abandoned. Also the tree-ring record shows that a number of very severe droughts occurred prior to the one between A.D. 1276 and 1299, yet widespread abandonments did not take place. However, it could be that the "great drought" was simply the last straw in areas that were already suffering from numerous other problems.

An alternative explanation is the suggestion that arroyo-cutting in the late thirteenth century drastically decreased the amount of usable farmland. Either drought conditions or prehistoric timber cutting (for building material, firewood, and clearing of agricultural fields) or a combination of both could have begun such a cycle of erosion. The loss of fields, due to gullying, has been harmful to Hopi farming in the twentieth century and might have been a severe problem in the past, but did it cause abandonment? The thousands of check dams and terraces built by the Anasazi are still effectively holding soil and preventing erosion after seven hundred years. The Anasazi seem to have been able to cope with the problem.

Abandonment has frequently been attributed to warfare, either with "hostile nomads" or with other Anasazi. The Navajo and Apache, traditional Pueblo enemies and the eventual occupants of most of the abandoned Anasazi territory, are most often identified as the "hostile nomads" in question. This is, in fact, unlikely. The ancestors of the Navajo and Apache entered the Southwest nearly two hundred years after most of the abandonments had taken place. Then too, before the introduction of the horse by Europeans, nomads would not have been much of a threat to the Anasazi villages. Small groups of hunters and gatherers, without horses to enable them to carry out swift surprise attacks, would have been no match for the large and well-organized populations of the Anasazi pueblos.

Other writers have argued that warfare might have broken out among the Anasazi themselves. Though it is hard to imagine any people remaining in a state of constant peace, there is no direct evidence of widespread conflict. There are no burned villages and few skeletons with evidence of mortal wounds to lend credibility to the suggestion of major Anasazi wars. Short of actual warfare, factional disputes within Pueblo villages have caused their near abandonment in modern times. A well-known example is the tragic dispute that culminated in the split and near desertion of the Hopi village of Oraibi in 1906. Some scholars have proposed that similar disputes might have been the cause of prehistoric abandonments. Factional disputes are indeed common in small villages throughout the world, and they do sometimes lead to the breakup of the community. But among the Hopi and others, when such a sad event occurs, new villages are founded in the immediate vicinity. Unresolved factional struggles do not explain the abandonment of large regions.

Densely populated villages and poor sanitary practices can lead to epidemic disease. This has also been cited as a potential cause of abandonment. There is, unfortunately, little evidence to either substantiate or refute this idea, although the lack of large burial populations at most sites argues against it. Available skeletal remains sometimes show evidence of poor nutrition, but the infectious diseases that produce epidemics do not leave observable evidence on the skeletal remains.

Finally, it has been suggested that bad nutrition and declining birthrates may have greatly reduced the population and caused the saddened and discouraged survivors to leave. The evidence for this idea is ambiguous. A visible pitting or spongy texture found on some bones of Anasazi skeletons has been interpreted as possible evidence of poor nutrition and anemia. Yet modern clinical studies indicate that these conditions can be caused by a number of problems, such as a short but severe illness, that may not relate to the general health of the population.

Drought, arroyo-cutting, warfare, factionalism, and disease are among the most common reasons cited for abandonment. None has gone unquestioned as the single cause. A combination of factors, perhaps including some of these, is more likely to have been responsible.

New Thoughts On Abandonment

In the past four or five years, some archaeologists have begun to explore the question of abandonment from a different perspective. Rather than searching for a single cause, this approach considers patterns of abandonment that have occurred throughout the world, in both ancient and modern times. It also views abandonment in light of new, highly refined, and precise information about the past climate of the Anasazi Southwest.

In our own society we are accustomed to the long-term stability of settlements. Boston and New York have not become ghost towns despite the growth of Los Angeles and San Diego. London, Paris, Rome, and Athens have much longer histories. In the Near East the landscape is dotted with *tells*, or artificial mounds, representing the accumulation of villages over millenia. Yet in most of the Precolumbian Western Hemisphere, the abandonment of villages, towns, and cities was not uncommon. The great Mayan centers of Tikal, Palenque, and Chichén Itzá; the huge Mississippian settlements of Cahokia in East St. Louis and Kinkaid on the lower Ohio River; and thousands of other sites throughout North America and Mesoamerica were abandoned before Europeans ventured to the Americas. On a worldwide basis, perhaps the long-term stability of population centers is a greater mystery than is the pattern of abandonment.

Tree-ring studies suggest that even quite large Anasazi pueblos were rarely occupied for more than about eighty years; smaller sites were in use for much shorter periods of time. As long as land was plentiful, problems arising from the depletion of resources, such as firewood, seem to have been met by simply moving on. It is true that in historical times Pueblo Indians were known to have traveled nearly two hundred miles on hunting and gathering expeditions. When resources are needed daily, however, as is firewood for heating and cooking, long-distance expeditions become a greater burden than the effort involved in moving to a new location.

There is also a common Anasazi pattern in which small areas were abandoned one or more times during the period of prehistoric occupation. In such cases, there is rarely a mystery to explore; the people simply moved to neighboring areas. Minor climate changes have often been cited as the cause for these short-distance moves to slightly higher or slightly lower elevations, where conditions for crops were more favorable.

The prehistoric abandonments of larger regions, such as the Mesa Verde area or the San Juan Basin, are more complex and not necessarily the result of an accumulation of smaller residential moves. In case of Chaco Canyon, abandonment followed a period of population growth and a later period of decaying social integration. Older ties of trade broke down, and formal, planned villages and towns gave way to more casual architecture. In the Mesa Verde case, abandonment occurred after an increase in population and a decrease in the labor being invested in domestic architecture. In these areas, tree-ring studies suggest that the social disruptions coincided with a period during which rainfall became less predictable from one year to the next. Perhaps the older social solutions to the problems of spotty rainfall and droughts became less effective; it became more difficult to count on surplus crops to store and distribute to those who would otherwise go hungry.

The actual depopulation of vast areas of the ancient Anasazi homeland was probably due to a combination of factors: more variation in summer rainfall than had occurred in the past, the depletion of wood supplies for heating and building material, and the failure of the social ties of trade, exchange, and ceremonial sharing to provide for the people's needs. With life becoming more difficult, it is likely that factional disputes broke out more often. As a result some people sought homes with relatives and friends in distant villages. Possibly too, disputes between villages occurred over access to farmland or firewood, and, again, some of the people may have left to seek their fortunes elsewhere.

The abandonments seem to have been gradual, almost leisurely. Perhaps at first only the younger people or young couples with small children sought a better life in the new villages founded along the northern Rio Grande tributaries, the Upper Little Colorado River drainage, the Hopi Mesas, and the Zuni Plateau. Soon these areas boasted large settlements that were undoubtedly centers of active social and religious life and important links in new networks of trade and exchange. These areas became attractive places, drawing immigrants from many parts of the region. How would it have been to be among those who stayed in the old homeland and watched friends and children leave; to know that there were fewer people to help with the daily work, fewer visitors bringing trade goods, gossip, and news; and to realize that soon there would be too few people to hold the important ceremonies that marked the passage of the seasons? Surely the bonds of kinship and fellowship and the need for a rich and secure social life outweighed the sadness of leaving ancient homes.

Pathways to the Present

During the fourteenth century, very large villages were built along the Chama River, Rio Grande, Upper Little Colorado River, Rio Puerco, Pecos River, and in the highlands of central New Mexico and Arizona. These villages were certainly founded by a combination of local residents of long standing and migrants from the areas that had been abandoned. Many of these villages are considered ancestral sites by the modern Pueblo Indians. Puye, for example, is one of the ancestral villages of the modern Santa Clara Pueblo on the Rio Grande. Atsinna and Kawikku are among the ancestral Zuni pueblos, and the Homolovi ruins and Nuvoqueotaka, or Chavez Pass ruin, are ancestral Hopi sites. There is little mystery about who the descendants of the Anasazi are; they are the modern Pueblo Indians.

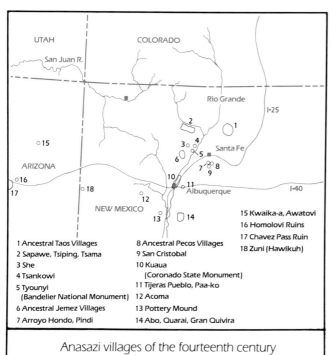

1 Ancestral Taos Villages
2 Sapawe, Tsiping, Tsama
3 She
4 Tsankowi
5 Tyounyi
  (Bandelier National Monument)
6 Ancestral Jemez Villages
7 Arroyo Hondo, Pindi

8 Ancestral Pecos Villages
9 San Cristobal
10 Kuaua
  (Coronado State Monument)
11 Tijeras Pueblo, Paa-ko
12 Acoma
13 Pottery Mound
14 Abo, Quarai, Gran Quivira

15 Kwaika-a, Awatovi
16 Homolovi Ruins
17 Chavez Pass Ruin
18 Zuni (Hawikuh)

Anasazi villages of the fourteenth century

The fourteenth-century villages differ from the old Kayenta, Mesa Verde, and Chaco settlements and differ from the pueblos of today. Some of the fourteenth-century villages were great, sprawling places. Sapawe, a fourteenth-century site on a small tributary of the Chama River, is the largest adobe ruin in New Mexico. It consists of more than one thousand rooms in multiple roomblocks, several large plaza areas, and many kivas. Chavez Pass ruin, near Winslow, Arizona, consists of more than one thousand rooms arranged in three primary roomblocks. Parts of this site were a single story, but other sections were two- and three-stories high. In the Zuni area, many fourteenth-century sites contained more than one thousand rooms constructed in multistoried roomblocks. The roomblocks were arranged around internal plazas and often had outer encircling walls. While the Chaco towns were planned and highly formal arrangements of rooms, plazas, and kivas, the fourteenth-century sites exhibit a different kind of planning. Many of these sites were built with an eye toward growth. The formal symmetry of the Chacoan towns did not permit rooms to be added easily as families expanded or new members joined the community. By contrast the fourteenth-century sites often consist of long rows of two or three tiers of rooms, to which another few rows or tiers could easily be added. There seems to be a great feeling of freedom and expansion at these sites. This contrasts sharply with both the monumentally formal Chaco structures and the confined Kayenta and Mesa Verde cliff dwellings that had been built a century or more before.

It is not surprising that the fourteenth-century villages departed from the older forms; even though much of the ancient Anasazi way of life had been retained, many of the old ways of doing things had failed, and organization had been irrevocably disrupted. Then too, new forms of organization were needed during this period of widespread population migrations. When people migrate to a new area, they rarely move as a single group. Studies of migrations on a worldwide basis, including studies of population movements among Pueblo Indians in historical times, indicate that the most frequent pattern is for a family group or a very few closely related families to follow separate migration paths, joining communities where they have ties of kinship or friendship. Among all of the modern Pueblos, origin and migration legends are important aspects of traditional lore. These legends invariably describe how different groups of people came together from different regions, sometimes separating for a time and sometimes being joined by other groups, until a highly complex web of intermingled elements became the modern pueblo. These legends reflect precisely those complex splittings and reorganizations that are common among people who have migrated.

Once the new villages were founded and had begun to grow, different trade networks were established and novel forms of integration were formed among them. Eastern Anasazi groups ventured through the passes of the southern Rocky Mountains and moved eastward toward the Great Plains. Trade between the Pueblo Indians and Plains Indian tribes developed and remained strong until well into the nineteenth century. Buffalo meat and hides from the Great Plains were exchanged for corn and sometimes pottery. Beginning in the fourteenth century, Pueblo pottery from the Rio Grande Valley began to appear in Plains Indian camps in Texas and Oklahoma. Some of the Rio Grande Pueblos adopted Plains Indian hunting and social dances with costumes that included bison hides and beadwork.

After their northern settlements were abandoned, the Pueblos of the fourteenth and fifteenth centuries seem to have increased their level of interaction with their neighbors to the south in what is now northern and perhaps central Mexico. More macaw skeletons have been found in archaeological sites dating from this period than from any preceding time. Some archaeologists suggest that the colorful, elaborate, and dramatic *Kachina* rituals may have entered the Southwest from Mexico at this time.

The *Kachinas* are specific spirit deities who are represented by masked impersonators on certain religious occasions among the modern Pueblo Indians. Kiva murals and rock art from the fifteenth century contain the earliest known depictions of *Kachina* figures. These figures have been found at archaeological sites from the Rio Grande west to the Hopi Mesas. This spatial distribution hints at the richness of ties among the villages at this time. Active exchange networks and social ties are also indicated by the great similarity in pottery recovered from sites throughout the Anasazi world during this period. The decorated pottery is often polychrome, black on yellow, or black on red. The colors and motifs, which include dancing figures, bird wings, and feather designs, again exhibit a freedom and sense of motion that differs markedly from the rigid geometric patterns manufactured during the preceding period.

At the turn of the sixteenth century the Pueblo world was thriving, active, and growing. Acres of lush green fields surrounded the villages. Cotton was dyed in vibrant hues and woven into kilts, dresses, cloaks, and sashes. Corn was ground, as it had been for centuries, on flat metates, and it was stored in granary rooms within the villages and also in brightly painted jars. Then, as today, dances held for the good of all the people were probably an occasion to visit with people from other villages. Guests would have brought gifts of food, pottery, and cloth to the village hosting the dance. At dawn, to the sound of flutes, drums, and chanting voices, elaborately costumed dancers would emerge from the kiva and enter the village plaza. There they would form their lines and begin the intricate patterns of the dances, as villagers and guests watched from the plaza edge or from rooftops overlooking the ceremony. With only brief periods of rest, groups of dancers would alternate dancing throughout the day. At sunset, after final prayers, dancers, villagers, and guests would feast and talk late into the evening within the pueblo rooms.

Perhaps the evening talks were of the old, long-abandoned villages, but there must also have been lively discourse about the future. Perhaps the hunts of winter were planned, or the next trading expedition to the plains was organized, or marriages were arranged, or the expected births of children were announced. No one could have known how very different the lives of those unborn generations would be, how forever altered the Pueblo world would soon become.

The Franciscans established a mission at Pecos Pueblo in 1620. It was destroyed during the Pueblo Revolt but later rebuilt. The restored eighteenth-century church at Pecos echoes some of its former grandeur. Pecos National Monument

The church at Pecos National Monument

At the easternmost edge of the Pueblo world, the Spaniards established the mission of San Buenaventura at the pueblo of Las Humanas. Abandoned by the Indians in 1675, the site today is called Gran Quivira. Salinas National Monument

Saint's Day procession, January 23,
San Ildefonso Pueblo

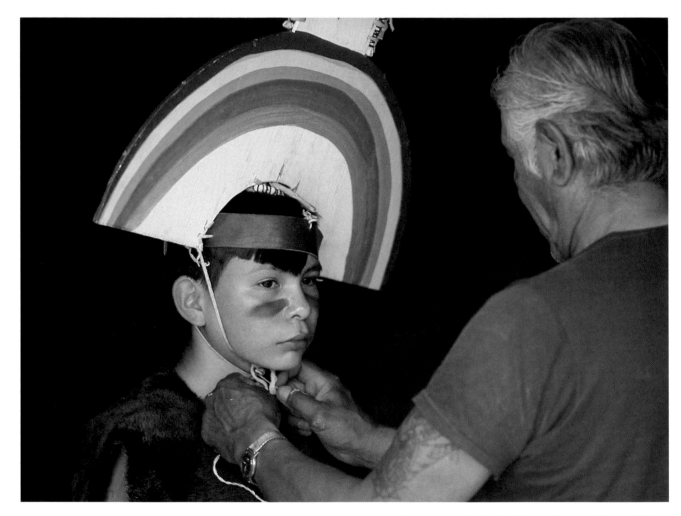

Preparation for the Rainbow Dance at Puye Cliffs,
ancestral site of the present-day Santa Clara Pueblo

Pueblo Indians guard a way of life that
is rich in ancient tradition.

Young dancer receiving communion during
Mass at Puye Cliffs

Taos Pueblo

Reflective pause on Feast Day,
San Ildefonso Pueblo

Pueblo Indians participate fully in modern American life. At the same time, the beauty of ritual that has been part of their way of life for millenia is carried into the future.

A deer dancer for tomorrow

Deer Dancer, Feast Day,
San Ildefonso Pueblo

Let us guard the Anasazi
legacy for all of the
children of the future.

Ricky Montoya of
Santa Clara Pueblo helps
prepare his family's
booth at Puye.

The Coming of Europeans

In 1540 Francisco Vásquez de Coronado led his expeditionary troops from Compostela, Mexico, into the Pueblo Southwest. These first Europeans to enter the Pueblo world were seeking both the fabled wealth of the "Seven Cities of Cíbola" and vast numbers of souls to baptize. The expedition made its way first to the Zuni villages. Then one party went on to the Hopi villages, while another went to Acoma, the Rio Grande pueblos, and Pecos. Dispirited by the lack of mineral wealth, the expedition spent the winter of 1541 near what is now the town of Bernalillo on the Rio Grande. In the spring they again ventured to Pecos. Some men were sent to Taos for supplies. Others journeyed far out onto the Great Plains, where they became distrustful of their Indian guide, killed him, and returned to the Rio Grande Valley. The situation worsened as the troops threatened mutiny, and finally in the spring of 1542, Coronado returned to Mexico. Although no Spanish expedition made its way to the Pueblos until 1581, the people were not left in peace with their land and their gods.

Portion of a Navajo pictograph at Standing Cow Ruin in Canyon de Chelly. A padre and conquistadores are among the figures represented.

The Spanish expeditions, even those that were simply charged with exploration, created difficulties for the Pueblos. Generally the parties consisted of only a few soldiers and priests, but these people were accompanied by their numerous Mexican Indian servants and retainers. Unlike modern armies, the exploring parties lived on provisions taken from the Pueblos. If the Pueblos refused to give food to the Spaniards, they were severely punished. In one such instance in 1582, members of the expedition led by Francisco Sanchez Chumascado burned a village near present-day Bernalillo. Some of the Indians were killed, trapped inside the burning rooms. Sixteen Indians who escaped the flames were then garroted and shot.

The strange, pale, bearded men riding horses (animals never before seen in the Pueblo world) brought some changes that even they did not understand. Perhaps the first, and most cruel, result of the Spanish *entrada* was recurrent disease and death. The Indians, having no immunities to European diseases, suffered devastating epidemics and high mortality. As late as 1853, an epidemic of smallpox reduced the Hopi First Mesa population from 1200 to 650 in only nine years. At least sixty-one pueblos are known to have been abandoned after 1540, many because of illness and population loss. These tragic losses must have had profound effects on the Pueblo economy and social organization. There may not have been enough able-bodied people to plant and harvest the crops or men who were strong enough to pursue the hunt. Some villages may have been unable to perform traditional ceremonies, because there were not enough people to carry out important roles. Villages that could not continue to survive socially may have joined other villages, as did

the few remaining inhabitants of Pecos Pueblo who moved to Jemez Pueblo in the nineteenth century.

Some of the changes wrought by the Spaniards were extensions of their colonial policies, and as such appeared reasonable to them. Conversion of the native people to the Roman Catholic faith was a primary goal of the colonial effort and one that was supported by a complex body of law and procedures. Before the codification of the *Law of the Indies* in 1680, it was legal to pursue Indian conversions by force if necessary. Not only were Indian religious practices prohibited but religious paraphernalia was confiscated and burned, and Indian religious leaders were tortured and killed. These barbarous practices turned native religious leaders into implacable enemies of the Spaniards, and the native religious practices were continued in secret.

Other official policies of the Spanish colonial effort involved conscripting Indian labor to build the missions. Some of the missions still stand as silent monuments to the Spanish vision of the glory of God and to Indian toil. At Pecos, Gran Quivira, Jemez, Abo, Acoma, and Quarai, the massive walls, graceful arches, and towers reproduced the appropriate form and order of seventeenth-century Roman Catholic religious design. The missions also introduced the Indians to valuable new products and technologies, such as domestic animals, the use of wool in textiles, and European crops such as wheat.

Two additional Spanish colonial policies were the *encomienda*, a grant of tribute the Indians had to provide, and the *repartimiento*, a system of conscripting Indian labor for Spanish farms, haciendas, and mines. These policies created tremendous hardships for the Indians. Although the Indians were to be paid a wage for their labor under the *repartimiento*, abuses were common and service was often cruelly enforced.

The impact of these policies was felt the most by the Pueblos along the Rio Grande, because they were closest to the Spanish capital of Santa Fe and the other Spanish colonial settlements. The Hopi villages were spared some of the repression, because they were too far away to be ruled effectively and because the barren landscapes of their mesas were not attractive to colonial farmers. Yet between 1629 and 1641, missions were founded at the Hopi villages of Awatobi, Shongopovi, and Oraibi, and the Hopi too experienced the cruelty of Spanish rule.

Finally in 1680, after years of hardship and repression, the Pueblos united in revolt against the Spaniards. The revolt was carefully planned; its chief strategist was a native leader from San Juan Pueblo, identified in documents as Popé. The plan, transmitted to all the Pueblos, was simple. On a specific day, every village would kill all the friars and settlers. However two Pueblo messengers, carrying final details of the plan, were captured, and the rebellion had to be put into operation one day prematurely. On 10 August 1680, the revolt took place. Twenty-one missionaries and approximately 380 settlers were killed. Missions, mission records, Spanish houses, government buildings, and haciendas were burned, and the remaining Spaniards were forced to abandon the Pueblo provinces and retreat into Mexico.

The Pueblo Indians kept the Spaniards out of their land for

Seventeenth-century Spanish missions of Arizona and New Mexico twelve years, but those years were a time of fear, disunity, and discouragement. Many villages were abandoned, and fortress strongholds were built on nearly inaccessible mesas and in the mountains. There was bickering and fighting among the Pueblos themselves. In 1681–82, in 1688, and again in 1689, the Spaniards tried, unsuccessfully, to retake the Pueblo area. In 1692 and 1693, Don Diego de Vargas led a military expedition that finally reconquered the New Mexican Pueblos, and missions were again established. The Hopi, however, successfully resisted the reconquest, and they were never again brought under Spanish domination.

From 1693 until 1821, when Mexico achieved independence from Spain, the Pueblo world was part of the Spanish Empire. At first, despite promises to the contrary, some of the Indian leaders of the Pueblo Revolt were executed by the Spaniards, and many colonial practices became as repressive as they had been before the rebellion. On 4 June 1696 a number of Rio Grande Pueblos and Pecos Pueblo again rose in revolt, but this uprising was not general or successful. By the end of the year peace was again restored. One group of Pueblos, referred to as the *Tano*, had long made their home in the Galisteo Basin south of Santa Fe. The Tano had occupied Santa Fe during the Pueblo Revolt of 1680 and participated in the uprising of 1696. They never again returned to their villages after this last, unsuccessful rebellion. Fearing Spanish reprisals, many of the Tano sought refuge among the Hopi. Their descendants reside today on the Hopi First Mesa.

After 1696 new laws and revised policies were enacted to curb some of the excessive cruelties of the early mission period, and colonists began to establish villages among the Pueblos. Very few of the colonists were of European or purely Spanish descent. Rather, most were the mixed descendants of Europeans and Mexican Indians who had been born in America. These Hispanic settlers used the Spanish language, followed Spanish customs, and embraced the Catholic religion. Increasingly through the years, Pueblo Indians and Hispanic settlers banded together for mutual protection against a new common enemy—fully mounted, nomadic Indian tribes. Although there is some dispute concerning the exact time of their arrival in the Southwest, Indians who were the ancestors of the present-day Navajo and Apache were living in the Pueblo area in the late sixteenth and early seventeenth centuries. Relations between the Pueblos and these newcomers seem to have been friendly at some times and mistrustful at others. During the Pueblo Revolt, many Navajo and Apache aided the Pueblos, and before the reconquest, the different Indian peoples lived in close proximity, often in the same villages.

After the reconquest and the establishment of many Hispanic villages, the incidence of Navajo or Apache raiding of settled communities increased. In part the problem arose because of a westward expansion of seminomadic Plains Indian groups. These Indians had been driven from their traditional lands by French and English colonists to the east. The Plains Indians probably obtained horses from the French. Once mounted, they possessed the ability to carry out quick raids on sedentary villages. The horse and the raiding economy eventually spread into the Southwest. The sedentary farmers, Pueblo and Hispanic alike, maintained stores of food that were prime targets for raiders, and they were raided by bands of Navajo, Apache, Kiowa, Comanche, and others.

Common interests and the need for protection drew the Pueblos and Hispanic colonists together. In some cases the compact Pueblo villages provided more security than did the Hispanic settlements. When parties of raiders threatened the Taos area, for example, the Hispanic villagers regularly sought refuge inside the walls of Taos Pueblo. Pueblo warriors were often recruited, supplied with horses and weapons, including firearms, and sent to fight as auxiliary troops in the colonial army. Pueblo troops were frequently commended for their bravery, and in many engagements they far outnumbered the colonials.

The Pueblo world was a truly remote and neglected outpost of the Spanish Empire. It took longer to send pack trains of supplies overland from Mexico City to Santa Fe than it did to send supplies from Mexico to the Philippines by sea. In the absence of adequate protection from the crown, and given the scarcity of European goods, Pueblos and Hispanic colonials became more dependent on each other. Hispanic colonists often used Indian-made pottery; planted their fields in corn, beans, and squash; and built their houses of adobe or jacal. The Pueblos acquired European farm animals and crops and a fluency in the Spanish language. Yet for all their interdependence, the two peoples, Pueblo and Hispanic, retained their separate identities and ways of life. For the Pueblo Indians, traditional wisdom, the ancient gods, ritual, and language are sources of strength to be cherished and guarded. Under Spanish rule the old ways were maintained in secret, as many are yet today.

During the mission period, Pueblo Indians were required to work as herdsmen, cowboys, smiths, and weavers for the Spanish authorities. In this way the Indians grew familiar with a variety of equipment, such as saddles, bridles, harnesses, metal axes, and knives. Some became highly skilled weavers and blacksmiths.

Spanish rule also effected changes in the political and religious life of the Pueblos. As they did throughout their empire, the Spanish authorities created a group of administrative officials in each village to implement their policies. These officials generally included a governor, his lieutenant, a "sheriff" charged with maintaining law and order, an assistant to the church priest, a superintendent for the irrigation ditches, and, after the Pueblo Revolt, a war leader and war captains under him. Although these offices must have been established among the Hopi during the early mission days, the Hopi were free of them after 1680, and no vestiges of them remain in Hopi political organization. Among the other Pueblos, these civil officials were later sanctioned by American authorities and continue to function in dealings between the Pueblo and the external governments. From the beginning, however, all the Pueblos retained their traditional leadership structure as well. The native leaders, generally the knowledgeable elders, are the *de facto* government; they see to it that the affairs of the pueblo are carried out, and they instruct the civil officials. Throughout the Spanish period, when religious persecution was always present, the civil officers served as a necessary facade behind which the

Church of San Geronimo, Taos Pueblo

native leaders functioned to maintain the Pueblo way of life.

The integration of Roman Catholicism into Pueblo culture has followed a similar pattern. Throughout the period of Spanish rule, attendence at the missions and church services was strictly required and at some times cruelly enforced. Yet the mission priests did not learn the native languages, and Pueblo understanding of the Catholic religion was minimal. Outwardly, the Indians were practicing Catholics, yet from the perspective of the church, they remained neophytes. Spanish religious authorities severely punished individuals who performed those traditional rituals that the church found offensive. This drove the Pueblos to carry out these rituals in closely-guarded secrecy. Some traditional ceremonies, considered benign by the church, were practiced frequently and openly, as though these were the only remaining vestiges of the traditional religion. Among the Rio Grande Pueblos, the summer *tablita*, or corn dances, are such occasions, and these are openly performed today. Among the Hopi, who escaped the more prolonged effects of Spanish repression, more varied, traditional ceremonial performances may be observed by outside guests. The Rio Grande Pueblos also adopted, and still openly perform, Spanish Catholic dances and ceremonies, such as the masked Matachina dances performed in honor of the Virgin Mary. Yet even in villages where both Catholic and traditional ceremonies are observed, there is no mixing or blending of native and Catholic ritual elements. Catholic rituals are performed free of native embellishments. The pure native religious ceremonies, without Catholic elaborations, are retained and performed only in complete secrecy.

In most of the Pueblo villages, the old mission structures were razed during the Pueblo Revolt and never rebuilt again. They may remain today as undistinguished piles of rubble outside the center of the village. The small modern Catholic church is an important place in the Pueblo village, though it stands as a separate structure, generally outside or at the farthest end of the plaza. It is located away from the core of village activity and away from the kivas. The Pueblo insistence on separation of alien and traditional ways enables them to maintain their cultural values, their traditional knowledge, their languages, and their beliefs.

The Pueblos developed their ways of adapting to European rule—conceptual separation of elements among the Rio Grande Pueblos, Acoma, Laguna, and Zuni and rejection of foreign elements among the Hopi—during the long Spanish colonial period (1693–1821). Following Mexican independence from Spain in 1821, the land of the Pueblos became part of the Republic of Mexico, but the methods used to adapt to the rule of foreigners remained much the same. One of the seemingly enlightened policies of the Mexican government worked to the detriment of the New Mexican Pueblos, however. Within the Mexican state, the Indians were given full citizenship, including the right to sell and dispose of land. Although pueblo boundaries were, in theory, guaranteed by treaty, there were numerous abuses and disputes. Hispanic settlements encroached on Pueblo lands; some Pueblo land was appropriated and some was sold.

When the Americans took possession of the Pueblo territory in 1846, the Pueblos continued to apply many of the same tactics of adaptation to foreign rule that they had found useful for centuries. There have, of course, been many changes in the Pueblo world since then, and the pace of change has increased. Early American government policy toward the Pueblos was extremely repressive. Official policy, carried out by the United States Indian Bureau, was designed to "Americanize" the native Americans. There was continued religious persecution. Under the Religious Crimes Code, traditional Indian religious activities were prohibited, and those who attempted to maintain native belief systems were persecuted. There was also a new strategy aimed at weakening the ties between Pueblo children and their native cultures. Boarding schools, which Pueblo children were required to attend, were deliberately located far from the villages; frightened, alone, and deprived of their families' support, these children were forced to learn the English language and American ways. Since the 1930s, however, more enlightened policies have been implemented, and Pueblo Indians have had much greater autonomy and a voice in their own affairs. Most of the Pueblo villages have adopted their own constitutions; schools are located in the villages; and freedom of religion is provided for by law.

The ability to maintain a separation between traditional and foreign ways has permitted the Pueblos to adapt to the various powers that have invaded their world. To the casual observer, Pueblo culture may seem to be an unsystematic mixture of traditional and nontraditional elements, but this is far from the case. By maintaining a mental and physical separation of these traditional and nontraditional elements and by cherishing a powerful respect for the past, the Pueblos have retained their traditional languages, their religions, and their values while participating in all areas of modern American life. They engage in the professions, industry, and trades, yet their identity as Pueblos is of utmost importance. The white man's time on the Pueblo land has been short. In the long-term scheme of time and the land, Anglo-American ways have barely been tried. The traditional Pueblo Indian ways have enabled a people to survive the millenia. The Pueblo values are guarded, nurtured, cherished, and instilled in each new generation.

The present-day Pueblo villages and the ancient Anasazi towns are testimony to a remarkable people. The Pueblo Indians have met the challenges of a harsh environment; when they faced insurmountable obstacles, they abandoned their once thriving villages and rebuilt their society in new lands. They have adapted to the incursions of foreign peoples and the imposition of alien ways by preserving traditional values. Their success reflects resilience in the face of change.

Cliff Palace, Mesa Verde

Dwellings of tuff,
Bandelier National Monument

Mummy Cave, Canyon de Chelley

Acoma Pueblo,
the oldest continuously
inhabited town
in the United States

Petroglyphs, Galisteo Basin, New Mexico

Hovenweep National Monument

Part of the enduring landscape,
Shiprock seen from Mesa Verde

DEWITT JONES has been a photographer and filmmaker for the past fourteen years. His photographic essays have appeared in *National Geographic* magazine, and his films have been twice nominated for Academy Awards. His books include *John Muir's America; Robert Frost: A Tribute to the Source; What the Road Passes by;* and *Visions of Wilderness.* Mr. Jones makes his home in Bolinas, California.

LINDA S. CORDELL, professor and chairman of the Department of Anthropology at the University of New Mexico, has been teaching and directing research in Anasazi archaeology for fourteen years. Her field projects have included excavations at Tijeras Pueblo, Rowe Ruin, and Teypama Ruin. Her books include *Tijeras Canyon: Analyses of the Past,* and *Prehistory of the Southwest.* She is also the author of many scholarly publications.